T

MAN'S GREAT FUTURE

by ERWIN D. CANHAM

AWAKENING: The World at Mid-Century

NEW FRONTIERS FOR FREEDOM

MAN'S GREAT FUTURE

Edited by

ERWIN D. CANHAM

Condensed by

ROD NORDELL

From the 50th Anniversary Edition
of *The Christian Science Monitor*

LONGMANS, GREEN AND COMPANY
New York · London · Toronto

1959

LONGMANS, GREEN AND CO., INC.
119 WEST 40TH STREET, NEW YORK 18

LONGMANS, GREEN AND CO., LTD.
6 & 7 CLIFFORD STREET, LONDON W I

LONGMANS, GREEN AND CO.
20 CRANFIELD ROAD, TORONTO 16

MAN'S GREAT FUTURE

PUBLISHED SIMULTANEOUSLY IN THE DOMINION OF CANADA
BY LONGMANS, GREEN AND CO., TORONTO

FIRST EDITION

LIBRARY OF CONGRESS CATALOG CARD NUMBER 59-14398

Printed in the United States of America
VAN REES PRESS • NEW YORK

CONTENTS

22018

INTRODUCTION

THE MAGNIFICENCE AND THE DANGER OF AN AWAKENING WORLD
gave *The Christian Science Monitor* the materials that make
up this book. We have mobilized the writing resources of a
global staff and turned to outside technical authority when
needed.

Two intertwined—almost synonymous—themes run through
all we have written. They are progress and freedom. This
volume is a chronicle of progress. But it is also a trumpet call
for freedom. It is essential that progress shall lead to freedom.
Men must not forge new shackles for themselves. As they
attain mastery over material elements, they must not fall
victims to materialism. Thus a note of constant warning and
danger runs through the triumph of the time.

The first section, "Freedom of Space: A New Vision Beckons," acknowledges the challenge of the space age as perhaps
the supreme paradox of our time. Shall our leap out into space
be used for the benefit of mankind, in fabulous new knowledge and relationships, or shall it be used to seek to enslave
human society under planetary bombardment directed from
space platforms or satellites? Shall this greatest new area of
knowledge lead us forward or backward? To explore the possibilities and the dangers of the new world of space is the task

of this first section. We do it factually, soberly, but graphically. It may well be the major theme of human thinking on cosmic affairs for the *next* fifty years—at least.

The title of the second section, "Awakening of Peoples: Abdul Listens to Tomorrow," tells its own story. And here color abounds, for we tell of the exuberant student in Ghana, the newly land-owning farmer in Japan, and many another whose life is bursting with new freedom. People are awakening everywhere, in old societies or new. The most explosive force in today's world is not the hydrogen bomb, but the released potentialities of people. It is their story we seek primarily to tell. For the years to come, whatever they may hold of space exploration, will surely be the age of awakening peoples. The sun has already risen, and the day is well advanced.

Then, in the third section, "Man and Nature: More Triumphs Ahead," we explain the essence of this awakening as it affects man's new capacity to control and dominate his material environment—a great fact of the time. Translated from terms of kilowatts and megatons, this becomes machines to wash the dishes more effectively. Or, as in India, a simple device to convert the power of one or two bullocks into electric lights for a whole village. Or, as in many Western countries, the effect on human living of the car, the television, and the school. These three are only symbols, but they represent a tremendous widening of human horizons. They, too, are explosive forces with an impact far deeper and wider than bombs.

To buttress and safeguard these great new freedoms we turn in the fourth section, "Man's Relation to Man: Freedom for Spiritual Unfoldment," to examining the degree to which new knowledge of the nature of matter and of the universe— the ferment of learning which sweeps humankind—also car-

ries with it a growing spiritual awareness. Perhaps the signs
are still tentative, but to the discerning eye they are inevitable. At the heart of the new knowledge there lies the doom
of materialism. The facts of modern life speak impellingly of
the urgency of love and brotherhood. The spark of freedom
within man has burst out in dark corners lately. His God-
given spiritual status ultimately saves his society. In this
section, we have surveyed the status of the arts. They, too,
show the irrepressible flame within man bursting into form
—clouded or clear.

Finally, in the fifth section, "Nations Living Together:
Potentials for Peace," we survey the immediate problem of
the time: the threat of global war. We examine the best
available information on the military situation—is there
a nuclear stalemate?—and trace the paths which may lead to
enforceable agreements to reduce the dangers of war and to
preserve peace. Our correspondents, who must concentrate
day in and day out on this evidence, have distilled their
expertness into clear analyses of the situation and the prospects.

Here, then, is a five-part survey which summarizes the
available data on the age into which humankind is moving.
This is the *Monitor's* response to the needs of its readers, and
of a wide public, at this moment in history. It should serve
as a challenge to thinkers. All too great is the evidence of
apathy, and of the acceptance of false materialist values in
many parts of the world. Nowhere is this somnolence more
menacing than in the United States. For the American people
bear heavy responsibilities in the latter-day world.

And upon American life in the last decade there has
descended a pall of complacence which has been only partly
shattered by the launching of the Soviet sputniks and the recession of 1957-58. Has awakening truly come? The most

candid observers cannot assure us that it has. The sputniks warned us that the Soviet Union had attained a strength in the missile field which gravely threatened the free-world security. The recession showed that economic stability and virility had not yet been assured in the domestic economy. But the edge of the sputnik warning wore off and recovery from the recession set in.

Underneath, however, the warnings remain as grave as ever—and the need for awakened citizenship as urgent. The pervasive tone of this book, dedicated to progress and freedom, is manifestly optimistic. But the optimism is based upon one prerequisite: that citizens remain alert and responsive to their total civic responsibilities. What are some of these? What is our unfinished business? A thumbnail list would include:

The need to preserve the peace, transitionally by means of adequate military power but fundamentally by reducing the misunderstandings between peoples which produce armaments and war.

The need to understand the true nature of free society—both political and economic—as people in the Western world have sought to live it during their best moments, and to make this nature clear to the uncommitted peoples.

The need to share and exemplify the practical knowledge which is helping to free people from enslavement to matter.

The need to clarify man's dedication to spiritual values, and to live it.

The need to apply this clarification to the urgent problems of civic affairs, as in the necessity for better schools, rebuilt cities, decency and honesty in government at all levels.

The need to help preserve the individual from the pressure of mass-ism in an age of mass production, mass distribution, mass communication.

The need to stem the tides of statism, whether communist, fascist, socialist, or whatever, and to stir the individual—and the individual nation—to the fullest possible solution of his own problems for himself.

The need to utilize fully the values of voluntary collective action, when the individual is helpless alone, before turning to the state or to compulsory association.

The need to open channels of communication by which the misunderstandings which prevail between the peoples of the free world and of the Communist world can be reduced.

The need, urgent for Americans, to reduce the all-too-prevalent misconception that they are dedicated only to material goals, that their society is tasteless and immoral, and that they are unfit for world responsibilities. Other misunderstandings prevail between other peoples.

The need to demonstrate bolder, more courageous and imaginative leadership in all the free societies.

The need, also urgent for Americans but needed by all, to respect the dignity and honor of all individual men everywhere, recognizing their aspirations and according them their full stature as sons of God.

The need to believe and act upon the tenets of free society with even more zeal and skill and persistence than the Communists devote to Marxism.

These are among the deeper duties of citizenship. They are presently unfulfilled. In the face of such challenges, how can any citizen be complacent?

If this volume, like the special newspaper edition which preceded it, helps to awaken thinkers to more effective acceptance of their responsibilities, through a better understanding of the facts and their meaning, it will have been the best possible contribution *The Christian Science Monitor* could make to the world on its golden anniversary.

This book has been condensed by Rod Nordell from *The Christian Science Monitor*, Fiftieth Anniversary Edition, edited by Harry B. Ellis. The writers are Dorothy Adlow, Jessie Ash Arndt, John Beaufort, Robert R. Brunn, Robert C. Cowen, Saville R. Davis, Bicknell Eubanks, Earl W. Foell, William R. Frye, Geoffrey Godsell, Robert M. Hallett, Joseph G. Harrison, Henry S. Hayward, Kimmis Hendrick, Helen Henley, Harold Hobson, Albert D. Hughes, John Hughes, Harry C. Kenney, Melvin Maddocks, John Allan May, Betty D. Mayo, Edwin F. Melvin, Carlyle Morgan, Tully Nettleton, Rod Nordell, Francis Ofner, Takashi Oka, Ernest S. Pisko, Richard W. Porter, Donovan Richardson, Harold Rogers, Sharokh Sabavala, Courtney Sheldon, Ronald Stead, Edmund Stevens, William H. Stringer, Emilie Tavel, Millicent Taylor, Gordon Walker, John C. Waugh, Nate White, and Paul Wohl.

—ERWIN D. CANHAM

MAN'S GREAT FUTURE

FREEDOM OF SPACE

A New Vision Beckons

1.

MAN'S GREAT FUTURE IS MORE THAN A PIOUS PHRASE. IF THE future is great with hope, it is also great with challenge, great with complexity. How can the individual of today effectively meet his awesome tomorrows?

Nowhere is the question posed more spectacularly than in man's expanding domains in space. The journey outward to the stars demands a journey inward to the mind and heart. It might begin as casually as this:

"Hey, you in Spaceracer J-303, where do you think you're going? This is Interstellar Traffic Control."

"Sorry, officer! We're heading for Proxima Centauri. Will you give me the right course, please?"

"You want Spaceway 66. You're 80,000 miles off. Turn one degree left and you should pick it up in five minutes. Correct bearing is zero, four, five. Be sure to hold it or you'll be tangling with cross traffic between Venus and Mars about 20 million miles out."

This could easily be your grandson's first encounter with the law. Note the officer said nothing about speeding. That's because the limit is automatic—670 million miles per hour. Even that souped-up, supercharged photon rocket Junior is riding cannot exceed the speed of light—its own power source.

Sounds fantastic, doesn't it? But hardheaded natural scientists say it isn't. The more careful ones say it may be your great-grandson who will reach the stars and they think your son may have to be content with slower travel—say something under a million miles per hour. That will restrict him to mere interplanetary journeying. But he should be able to reach Mars and Venus in a few days—for they are a million times closer than the nearest stars.

And you? How far and fast will you go? The predictions are that you may reach no farther than the moon—a mean distance of 238,857 miles at 25,000 miles per hour, allowing for some slowing in starting and stopping. It is now expected that American scout rockets will take instruments around the moon within three years. Manned space travel is said to be less than a decade away.

Of course, where so many still unknown factors are involved, man's conquest of space cannot be calculated exactly.

But there is much to support the confident predictions. For the rate of man's conquest of his physical environment has been speeded beyond belief. From the oxcart and sailboat to the steamboat and locomotive was something like five thousand years; the next step, to the automobile and airplane, was approximately one hundred years; the next, to the atomic age, about forty; and the next, to the sputniks, only twelve.

Moreover, instantaneous communication has speeded the exchange and fructifying of knowledge. When Leif Ericson stumbled on the New World, later called America, few people learned of it. Centuries later Columbus thought he was the discoverer. But when Sputnik I reached the new world of space, news of the event circled the globe even faster than the satellite itself.

History has dealt harshly with doubters. The man who scoffed at the feasibility of steam railways "because the human system could never endure a speed of 30 miles an hour" was himself traveling many times as fast even while he spoke. For presumably he was on the crust of this fast-spinning orb, old earth. If he was near the equator he was doing nearly 1,000 miles per hour!

Of course progress has to be demonstrated. But daily it becomes clearer that it is a spiritual and mental process. Thought is the pioneer. Once self-imposed mental barriers begin to fall, astounding things happen. Human beings sometimes behave like the fish about which a story is told. When a glass partition was removed from their tank, they refused to go beyond the line where it had been. Only when some were forced across the accustomed boundary would they use the new space available.

Why go into space? Just to satisfy curiosity? No, although what is called curiosity may be connected with more respected qualities—the thirst to know, the desire to grow.

In Kipling's charming story, "The Elephant's Child," about how the elephant got his trunk, the young, short-nosed elephant's " 'satiable curtiosity" continually got him into trouble. It also won him valuable knowledge and a very useful trunk. So it has been with men. Their never-satisfied whats and whys have led them into countless hazardous adventures and great tribulations. But vast benefits also have accrued.

Space is only the latest last frontier. The youth who dreams of traveling to the stars is today's version of the caveman who wondered what lay beyond the hill and finally dared climb until he discovered a new world in the next valley. The unknown ever beckons. No perils, no failures, no timid logic ever prevails finally against the necessity to dream, to inquire, to seek, to test, to explore. Indeed, the recurrence of this pattern in human progress suggests something more fundamental than curiosity—something akin to a law of nature or of God.

Religious thinkers will see here once more the process of awakening, of man groping to realize his full stature as the image and likeness of God. Is not his struggle to break the limitations of time and space impelled by the fact that the true, spiritual man can no more be localized than can his Father, infinite Spirit? For many, this concept explains progress better than theories of material evolution do.

Better understanding of it could well smooth our path into space. It could help to eliminate much blind trial and error. For the awakening that spells progress need not be painful. There is no iron law which requires invention to be nine-tenths perspiration, one-tenth inspiration. The great discoveries, the so-called inventions, have entailed only recognition and utilization of hitherto unperceived powers, properties, and possibilities. Who wants to put a limit on the good that space can hold?

The space age has opened so suddenly that most of us are barely beginning to look for its possibilities. In many a home you can hear a conversation something like this:

"Why are you so fascinated by this space stuff, son? It's strictly for the birds. You'd do much better to dig into something practical—physics, chemistry, electronics. The country needs engineers."

"But, dad, all those things are tied in with space exploration. They are needed in it and it throws new light on them."

"Well, you don't catch me setting out for the moon in a plastic suit and with pills for food."

"Okay, dad, but some of the men who do will help make it possible for you to attend a bankers' meeting in Tokyo and get home the same weekend."

Here is one answer to the question, What can space do for us?

American taxpayers who are supplying several hundred million dollars for the work of a national space agency should be interested in practical applications.

At least four such uses are already in sight. As the boy said, one is travel. Work on manned space flight is closely connected with the development of rockets, which will be the next step beyond jet planes in shortening journeys right here on earth.

Another early use is foreseen in the speeding up of communications. For instance, television, limited by the horizon, now uses towers to obtain a wider range. Three satellites with transmission or booster facilities powered by solar batteries could extend TV's reach around the globe.

Tremendous value is expected from improved weather observations obtained from instruments lifted into space. It is hoped that within a few years weather maps many times as complete and accurate as today's can be made with the aid of satellites.

Finally come military uses. These go beyond the connection between the development of rocket power for space ships and for ballistic missiles. Reconnaissance from satellites with haze-piercing infrared cameras and other devices carried by satellites on known courses is an obvious first step. Machines which can "memorize" information and transmit it at chosen intervals by radio code are available.

Yet it was only a few decades ago that a British prime minister, trying to underscore the preposterous extremes of military demands, said: "The generals always want to fortify the moon!"

More attuned to today were the foresights of the founder of *The Christian Science Monitor*, Mary Baker Eddy, who wrote: "The astronomer will no longer look up to the stars,—he will look out from them upon the universe . . ." (*Science and Health with Key to the Scriptures*, p. 125.)

How will space affect our thinking? Some may seek in it escape from human problems. It will not provide that. But it can help to lead us into larger dimensions of thought which in turn can ease earth's conflicts. It should jolt us out of pettiness, put new meaning into Samuel Longfellow's "the wide horizon's grander view." Amid the galaxies there should be little room for tribalism and provincialism.

The first experience with space—the satellite launchings—happily occurred under the broad, nonmilitary auspices of the International Geophysical Year. Highly urgent are arrangements, possibly through the United Nations, to continue at least this degree of international cooperation. Failure holds all too obvious dangers—reckless military ventures involving the possibility of conflict. Satellites can be suspected of sky-spying, if not of containing stores of H-bombs ready for release. How high does a nation's air sovereignty extend? Under what rules can the new oceans of the sky be used? How about colonies?

To make full use of the new freedom of space, men will have to awaken, not merely to larger concepts of time and space, but to larger concepts of man. Otherwise, they will carry incongruously into the illimitable new world the little hates, greeds, fears, and passions which bedevil them in the old.

But we can free ourselves from these burdens as from any material limitation which cumbers progress. In the measure we come to understand our true heritage as the sons of God, the one Spirit which pervades and rules the universe, we shall prove big enough to enjoy wonders of His kingdom still unglimpsed in our dreams of space.

It is a thrilling yet sobering prospect, all this. Horizons, once opened, cannot be shut down. But it will be no quick conquest. The United States, its allies, its competitors, cannot overrun their technical limitations, the pace of their research, the limitations of budgets, the political understanding of their peoples.

The space conquest will be tremendously costly, running, it is estimated, into a trillion dollars, before a manned space ship roars majestically to Mars. Only a wealthy nation with an annual gross national product soaring beyond the 500 billion dollar figure could hope to enter this race. More likely, the project will be pooled among allies. Or perhaps a global space agency will eventually materialize under the aegis of the United Nations.

Make no mistake, the Russians have been at this a long time. Back in 1903 Dr. K. E. Ziolkowsky, of St. Petersburg, was blueprinting a liquid-propellant rocket motor. It is very evident, from the tremendous thrust of Soviet rocket motors already developed, that this interplanetary sport is to be keenly competitive.

Who will lead these peacetime explorations? One must sadly conclude that space expeditions will not have much use for those grand individualists, the dynamic pioneers who trekked by dog team to the poles, who first penetrated darkest Africa, who scoured the Gobi Desert. The new emphasis is on teamwork and technology.

Physicists, engineers, men with Ph.D.'s and Phi Beta Kappa keys, competent with computers, familiar with mathematical formulae, brilliantly aware of the new metallurgy and the arcane vistas of nuclear science, operate with lavish equipment, their research and development backed by governments or the great foundations.

With mathematical precision, testing minutely as they go, they advance into the intricate unknown.

Yet they, too, and those who watch, dream dreams as breathtaking as those hatched by a Peary or a Stanley.

They will build a space station—a "way station" to the planets. From this platform they will look out clear-eyed across the universe, no longer peering by telescope through the murk of earth's wavy atmosphere.

2.

How will such a space station be launched? Here is one procedure based on facts already known.

The scene is space, 400 miles above the earth. A missile—several stories tall—has just joined two others in silent orbit.

As they hurtle on side by side 18,000 miles an hour, a weird drama begins. Two swept-wing gliders break from the nose of the last tall missile and spin away toward the neighboring towers.

Suddenly, four men, accoutered in the regalia of space, emerge from the two gliders to hang suspended, weightless, in orbit.

Firing small rocket pistols to propel themselves from missile to missile, they flit to the tops of the two big towers.

Quickly the nose cones are removed. The largest of the missiles, standing already empty, is made ready to receive a space station. The second, loaded with cargo, is emptied by long lines which stretch from man to missile.

Everything—men, missiles, gliders, cargo, and lines—fixed together in space, rushes on in orbit, sweeping in a gentle turn above the curving earth hundreds of miles below.

Thus, a manned satellite is established at the threshold of the stars.

That scene in the near vacuum world of space can be

played in our generation. The technology with which to do it is today within the grasp of men. The platform itself exists—an Atlas intercontinental ballistic missile, hewn hollow to receive men and instruments.

Krafft A. Ehricke, assistant to the technical director at Convair Astronautics in San Diego, and a commanding figure in the field of space flight, thinks he knows both when and how man could establish a platform in space.

When? Soon—within five years.

How? That's a more complicated story. But to hear it is to be caught up in a dramatic preview of man in orbit.

This is how it would be on an Ehricke-designed satellite:

Its establishment in space will involve three modified Atlases, fired in staggered succession. From launching pads somewhere in the world, the first Atlas, its great hull empty, will be launched to 400 miles altitude and there, at its apogee, level off into a circular orbit. With propellant expended and its motors silenced, the huge vehicle will become a permanent cornerstone for the establishment of a space station.

It will be carefully tracked and its orbit pinpointed. Then a second Atlas, carrying 8,000 pounds of cargo and timed to the split second, will blast off. Fired aloft by an Atlas booster and kicked into final orbit by an upper-stage rocket, it will join the first Atlas in space.

The cargo vehicle will jockey to within a few feet of its predecessor in space, propelled by spurts from small control rockets.

Both missiles will orbit on, side by side, around the world. As they round earth and head again for their rendezvous point, the third Atlas, carrying on its nose the two manned gliders, will roar aloft and join its predecessors in orbit. Then will begin the weird ballet of man and missile in space.

The spacemen will drag their living quarters, a collapsible rubber nylon envelope, from the cargo ship and insert it in the nose of the waiting Atlas tank.

Fully inflated and pressurized it will contain four levels— a bathroom with shower at the tip of the nose, a galley and recreation room on the second level, a sleeping room on the third level, and, near the missile's midsection, a control room and space laboratory.

In the after half of the Atlas hull, spacemen will store their water, emergency power batteries, rocket propellant, tools, reserve equipment, and instrumentation. At its base will be clapped a shielded nuclear power plant. Aft on the Atlas hull will hang tanks of gaseous oxygen. Aft also on the Atlas sides will be fastened two gliders to be used as space life boats or for return of the crew to earth.

Small vernier rocket motors will send the platform tumbling end over end through space about two-and-a-half turns a minute. This will build up enough gravity—a tenth of a G— for the spacemen inside to know up from down, enough to make a 180-pound man weigh 18 pounds.

There will be no ladders from level to level in the satellite, just manholes. Spacemen weighing only 18 pounds can practically float from floor to floor.

An escape hatch drilled amidships will open to let crewmen enter and leave. The four spacemen will be able to crawl in and out through an air lock, stepping out if they wish for an occasional orbital stroll under the stars.

3.

Such stellar strolling will require the kind of detailed preparation with which fliers are already becoming familiar. Man is flying today at altitudes where conditions are little different from those he would face on an extended trip beyond the immediate environs of the earth.

That is why scientists of the United States Air Force School of Aviation Medicine at Randolph Air Force Base, San Antonio, Texas, have been studying the human factors of space travel for about a decade. They work under the guidance of Dr. Hubertus Strughold, German physician-philosopher, who has pioneered in space medicine and is world renowned as an authority on the subject.

In 1951, Dr. Strughold and his colleagues defined the "space-equivalent" levels for the human body within the earth's atmosphere at altitudes between 10 and 120 miles. In that year, the *Journal of Aviation Medicine* published a paper that was to become a classic research document.

Entitled, "Where Does Space Begin?" the paper was prepared by Dr. Strughold, Heinz Haber, Konrad Buettner, and Fritz Haber.

The paper points out that "the borders of space in relation to the earth are identified with those regions where the last traces of air become lost in the void, that is, 250 to 500 miles above the earth's surface; or, the borders of space are occasionally interpreted as that zone where the terrestrial field of gravitation is so reduced as to be insignificant."

However, it adds that this concept of space is "misleading when used in discussions related to manned rocket flight. Rather, these problems must be treated on the basis of the functions which the atmosphere has for men and craft."

"In this regard," the paper continues, "the atmosphere fulfills three important functions: the function of supplying breathing air and climate, the function of supplying a filter against cosmic factors, and the function of supplying mechanical support for the craft."

If one flies at an altitude where the atmosphere fails to

fulfill one or more of these functions, he has, for practical
purposes, begun to enter "space." Hence the concept of
"space-equivalent" flight, which Dr. Strughold and his staff
have investigated for many years.

These studies now are forming the basis of the new science
of space medicine, as the investigation of the physiological
and psychological aspects of space and near-space travel is
called.

It was also in 1951 that Major General Otis O. Benson, Jr.,
in his first tour of duty as commandant of the School of Aviation Medicine, remarked that fliers "frequently encounter
environments whose dimensions have not been charted with
any final accuracy."

Writing recently in the *Army-Navy-Air Force Journal*,
General Benson, on another tour of duty as the head of the
school, points out that the years since then were the period
in which the Air Force was converted from "the reciprocating
engine-powered aircraft of World War II into an all-jet
combat organization. In civil aviation, the transition to jet
transports is near at hand." More than that, according to
General Benson, the same period "has marked the beginning
of the next transformation in human flight, from jets to
rockets."

Man already is exploring regions where it never before
has been possible to make actual observations and carry out
research firsthand. From such tentative probings into space,
the Air Force teams are able to make the first actual checks
on what General Benson said were "reasonable deductions as
to the medical effects of such altitudes, based on information
gained by instrumental research vehicles, or on experiments
with low-pressure chambers and other apparatus."

The researchers begin with the problem of learning as
much as possible about an unknown area so the pilot can sur-

vive his first contact with it. Then they check what the pilot finds on his first test flights to assure the safety and efficiency of pilots on routine operational flights later on.

General Benson points out that the School of Aviation Medicine, through its Department of Space Medicine, was getting ready for the space-flight era long before man began actually to probe its limits.

General Benson and his research team are aware that the effects of even the thin upper atmosphere on the human body are serious problems. At present they are barriers to the final breakthrough into the void beyond the outer fringes of that atmosphere.

The general emphasizes that "we do not expose the flier to these conditions without the fullest possible protection. Our purpose in studying these problems is to overcome them."

Physiologists at the school and elsewhere also have devoted much study to what they call the "time of useful consciousness." In his article in the *Army-Navy-Air Force Journal*, General Benson describes this as "the period of grace that a flier has in which to take some remedial action, if he should be abruptly left without cabin pressure at very high altitudes."

He says it has been determined that this time drops to about 12 seconds at about 52,000 feet, or 10 miles, even for a pilot breathing pure oxygen. No matter how far a pilot goes beyond that into space, the time reserve stays just about the same.

General Benson explains that this is because, at the low pressures found anywhere above 10 miles, "the lungs are filled to their full capacity with carbon dioxide and water vapor. Hence, the flier cannot inhale any oxygen. Yet he has enough left in his blood and in his tissues to last him for about twelve seconds. And this will be true if he undergoes an explosive decompression even in the depths of space."

There are other problems which the research team has tackled with intense dedication. They include the effects on men of ultraviolet radiation, cosmic rays, heat radiation, the scattering of light, and the propagation of sound—not to mention the puzzling phenomenon of weightlessness. As physical phenomena, these problems are being studied in many research laboratories.

As the limits of space flight are extended farther out from the earth, men encounter these problems with increasing frequency. The Air Force describes space flight as operations in the region above 10 to 12 miles. Dr. Strughold himself is insistent that a sharp distinction be made between the terms "space flight" and "space travel."

Space *travel*, according to Dr. Strughold, or *interplanetary* flight, is a project for tomorrow. Space *flight* is taking place now in rocket-powered craft that rise for brief periods to the edge of the atmosphere and then return to the earth.

Researchers at Randolph, incidentally, have determined that the most feasible pressure to be maintained inside a cabin would be about half that at sea level—or the equivalent of about 18,000 feet altitude. Designing engineers say this is practicable from a structural point of view.

Other engineering problems to provide for normal human functions include removing excess carbon dioxide and water vapor exhaled by the crew, controlling the temperature raised by a flier's metabolism in closed environment, disposal of body wastes, and reusing waste fluids to avoid having to carry an original large supply of drinking water in the rocket vehicle.

Despite all these and other problems, the experts at Randolph insist that if they were asked to provide a livable cabin for a craft to operate in outer space, they could write the specifications which the engineers could meet. But, they add, the aim is not only to help the crew to survive. It is also to provide the most efficient unit to give the crew the best in safety, operational ease, and comfort as it goes into the unfamiliar environment of space.

Comic relief tinges the problems of space flight when the layman encounters the tricks of interplanetary time. When man starts traveling several hundred thousand miles per second, strange things are expected to start happening. At such high speeds time begins to "stretch," and, as velocity approaches the speed of light, time might even appear to stand still.

As one accelerates away from earth, earthly things fade. The four seasons become longer, minutes and hours become longer. The traveler himself will eat less often, sleep less, and even the pulse beat will slow down.

Light takes a million years or so to travel from here to the next big assembly of stars, or spiral galaxy. Yet, according to the men who are supposed to know, a space traveler may be able to get there in his lifetime. And the reason (simple, they say) is that what seems like a million years to one here on earth does not necessarily seem like a million years to another out in space (and here is the catch) if he travels fast enough.

If a man should travel from here to Andromeda, to the observer on earth he would seem to take more than a million years. And, when he goes to Andromeda and comes back, he will find that the earth has got older by more than two million years. Yet he accomplished it all in his own lifetime.

So, many people are now asking if a weekend trip into space would turn the years back. If a person took a trip into space, would he return younger, fresher, and gayer? You would think that it would be possible to get a yes or no answer to this. But, no sir! Several of the top physicists in

New York took a reporter on a universe grand tour on the subject without ever committing themselves.

However, one expert was willing to go part way out on the limb and it seems that, in "simplest terms," time would literally slow down for the person traveling in space at very high —but by no means improbable—speeds. As a result, a person traveling at two-thirds the speed of light would find upon his return from a trip to the star Sirius, brightest in our galaxy, that the journey had taken him five or six years less than his eighteen-year absence recorded on earth.

Now then, if you took the same trip would you come back five or six years younger? Relatively yes, when compared with an earth counterpart. Whether you would be older biologically is the hotly debated question.

But before all of this can happen to you, you will be happy to know that considerable research must be conducted into the necessary factors which will make your trip comfortable —not to say possible.

4.

The man in the manned space vehicle is being given every consideration, as we have seen. Research is also speeding ahead on the vehicle itself.

How will man fly? On the wings of what great propulsion systems will he ride?

How far into space will the big, noisy, high-thrust chemical rockets of today take him? Where and when will he begin riding the atom? At what point in space will he cull propulsive energy from the free radicals, the sun, and from arc heating?

These, and others, are dramatic questions. And astronautic specialists the world over are seeking answers.

What makes a missile fly?

Newton explained it three centuries ago when he said that for every action there is an opposite and equal reaction. This is the physical law on which propulsion hangs.

In practical terms this simply means that if you exert a force—ejected gases, for instance—at high velocity out the back end of a thrust chamber, you will get an equal and opposite force pushing against the chamber's front end. If a rocket happens to be attached to the front end, it is bound to get pushed ahead.

The only factor making one propulsion system differ from another is the method used to produce this reaction thrust.

Every propulsion system flying today uses chemicals—either solids or liquids. In a liquid engine such as that in the Atlas intercontinental ballistic missile, an oxidizer—liquid oxygen—is pumped into a thrust chamber, where it is mixed with a fuel—hydrocarbon. The two are ignited, shooting gases out the rear of the chamber at great velocity. There is an opposite reaction, and Atlas takes off.

In a solid system—notably the Polaris intermediate range ballistic missile—the fuel is solid, much like a cake of soap. When it is ignited, it also shoots hot gases out. And Polaris also takes off.

These two propulsion systems will be the first available for the leap into space. They are capable of delivering great thrust—millions of pounds, enough to push a missile to interplanetary heights.

Experts in the field of advanced propulsion believe that chemical rockets, perfected to a fine edge and powered by super fuels, can fly to the near planets—Venus and Mars—millions of miles away.

They will always be useful in lifting vehicles through the heavy pull of the earth's atmosphere. Their booming thrust and quick acceleration make them excellent for take-offs and landings.

But for missions ranging into unlimited space they will either require a staggering number of rocket stages, piled one atop the other, or complex refueling systems. Chemical missiles, such as Atlas, drink enough fuel in only two minutes to fill a railroad tank car.

So, say the experts, we must look soon to other propulsion systems.

At the present time two advanced systems are the apple of the astronautic eye—the atomic and the ionic. Both are considered highly feasible, practical, and imminent.

Nuclear fission rockets would have limited range. Jupiter and Saturn in interplanetary space would be about their limit. The ion rocket, on the other hand, could theoretically run the full scale of space, even to distant galaxies.

A nuclear rocket system could theoretically increase tenfold the payload weight of today's chemical missiles. And it could lift these huge payloads—many tons—with a single-stage rocket.

What is more, it could deliver prodigious thrust, more than twice that of its chemical counterpart. A round trip to Mars might take a chemical rocket three years. It would take a nuclear vehicle only a single year.

In the nuclear system an atom-splitting reactor heats a fluid—ammonia, helium, or hydrogen—to high temperature. The fluid evaporates and is blasted out the rear.

Chemical and atomic propulsion systems could always lift vehicles away from earth and out of the atmosphere. But in upper space the demands are different. A rocket needs less thrust and more staying power. Since space is a near void, just a simple push is enough to propel a rocket to incredible speeds. Further, a machine in interplanetary space must be able to cruise continuously for days and months.

An ion rocket could be propelled through the space vacuum thousands of miles an hour by only a few pounds of thrust. Instead of shooting gas from its chamber, it would emit electrified ion particles, generated perhaps by a nuclear reactor.

An ion rocket is considered imminently feasible. Propulsion experts, such as Mr. Ehricke, say it can be realized within the next two decades.

What of the other systems—solar, arc heating, and the mysterious free radicals? These are all possibilities, say propulsion specialists. But they have serious drawbacks.

A solar rocket would get thrust by collecting radiation from the sun with gigantic mirrors. It would utilize this radiation energy to heat hydrogen or helium and thrust it through nozzles at great speeds.

The free radical system—known in astronautics as "the mysterious dance of the free radicals"—would, like solar rockets, find power in outer space.

Radicals (very active fragments of molecules) high in space would be "fractured." In their frantic attempt to return to their original bodies, they would release great amounts of energy. If this energy could be captured, it could be translated into thrust.

Arc heating, quite simply, would involve generating an electrical charge and arcing it between two contacts to heat a fluid. The fluid, in turn, would be expanded through nozzles to produce thrust.

All of these systems produce extremely low thrust and are limited to interplanetary probes. Like the ion rocket, they just couldn't build up enough push to hoist a rocket out of the atmosphere.

They also must carry complex equipment to create their special types of energy. This means, Mr. Ehricke descriptively says, that in some systems "you find yourself dragging along acres of accessory equipment."

Photon drive and fusion are still as mysterious as the heavens themselves.

Photon power, says Mr. Ehricke, "is still so deep in the womb of basic research that we shall never see it in our generation."

Photon and fusion would be the aristocrats of the propulsion systems. It would be they, together with ion, that would take men to other galaxies. But they are still unborn and may be unworkable.

5.

Certain propulsion systems, however, *are* workable—as the post-sputnik, post-Explorer world well knows. An understanding of present achievements is important for understanding future possibilities.

A Washington, D.C., newspaper recently carried a letter from a lady asking how many school buildings and teacher training schools, not to mention additional pay for teachers, could have been provided with the money used for "that moon rocket."

If the writer of this letter reflected any substantial feeling that launching a rocket to explore the environs of the moon is a stunt, then scientists have failed to communicate to the general public one of the most exciting developments in all the recorded history of science. For space probes and artificial satellites are not flashy stunts designed by small boys grown up. Nor are they merely propaganda weapons, effective as they may be in this field.

Earth satellites, moon rockets, and the space vehicles to

come are a thrilling advance in scientific technique, a giant step forward, as significant for our times as the telescope was for its. To be sure, there may be implications of military value in the conquest of space, and one cannot discount the appeal of exploring the unknown, of "reaching for the moon." But primarily these space vehicles present mankind with an unparalleled opportunity to thrust aside the curtains which have concealed from him so much of the basic mechanisms which drive his universe.

Although we must think of school buildings, we cannot think in terms of school buildings *or* satellite launching vehicles, for satellites are making available to us priceless new knowledge that will add a whole new dimension to the education our young people are receiving. If it is to remain dynamic, our society must expand not only its educational plant but also its knowledge of the world in which that society exists.

The International Geophysical Year, whose program in the United States was planned and directed by the National Academy of Sciences with financial support from the National Science Foundation, marked the beginning of man's exploration of outer space. There had been previous rocket firings into the fringes of the earth's atmosphere, but the IGY rocket-sounding program, expanded on an international scale, and the advent of artificial earth satellites, represent by far the largest steps taken toward the scientific exploration of outer space and the planets.

To understand the vital importance of space vehicles to science, it is necessary to recall the familiar analogy of man as a creature living at the bottom of an ocean of turbulent air. This ocean—the earth's atmosphere—is both man's hope and despair, for while it protects him from harmful radiations originating in outer space, it is also a barrier to his understanding of that space.

Through the ages man has peered upward, first with the naked eye, next with the optical telescope, and now, too, with the radio telescope. But, though the scientist now can see outward to immense distances, and backward in time two billion years, the opacity of the earth's life-giving atmosphere hides from him much that is of interest and, in some cases, prevents direct observation of it at all.

In pursuit of this evasive knowledge scientists have climbed mountains, loaded aircraft and balloons with instruments, and devised elaborate ground equipment. These indirect methods, combined with a good deal of ingenuity, have provided a truly remarkable store of information about extraterrestrial particles and radiations. Now, however, high-performance research rockets and satellites enable scientists to place their instruments in and beyond the upper atmosphere and not only permit more direct measurements of space and upper air phenomena but also provide a new perspective of the earth and of the lower atmosphere.

Current studies of cosmic radiation made possible by these new tools give us a dramatic example of their value. Cosmic rays are electrically charged particles originating somewhere in outer space, which smash with extremely high energies into the atoms of air thinly populating the outer edges of the atmosphere. These sundered fragments in turn collide with other atoms in the atmosphere. Ultimately these collisions and interactions result in secondary cosmic rays reaching the earth, but the primary cosmic rays which began the process have, in the meantime, disappeared.

Prior to the age of research rockets and satellites, scientists learned a great deal about primary cosmic radiation through indirect observations, but even more remained a mystery.

Now, for the first time, it is possible to place a scientific laboratory above the masking atmosphere, there to make direct measurements.

High-altitude rockets are of the utmost importance as a research tool, and even are preferred when a rapid vertical sampling from ground level to the upper atmosphere is desired. Nevertheless, an artificial satellite has three intrinsic advantages over rockets and other conventional means of scientific inquiry: the satellite covers a much wider area; it covers a wide area in a relatively short time, and it is far more effective for gathering synoptic data.

This last advantage is particularly important to meteorology and a number of other fields. The use of precision ground observation stations affords the satellite a fourth advantage in that orbit measurements yield data which are significant with respect to measuring the shape and size of the earth, air density, and ion density.

Robert H. Goddard fired the first American liquid-propellant rocket in 1926. Today the use of rockets for scientific exploration is still in its infancy. Every launching is a pioneering step into the unknown. Success depends on the perfect functioning of literally thousands of complex and interdependent parts. The accuracy requirements of velocity and guidance are exceedingly demanding.

It is small wonder, then, that not every attempt to launch an artificial satellite is successful. We are only on the threshold of space, at a stage of development which may someday be thought of as comparable to the Wright Brothers at Kitty Hawk or Henry Ford tinkering in his barn.

As Professor A. C. B. Lovell, director of the famous radio telescope near Jodrell Bank, England, has noted, decades of argument and uncertainty about the nature of the solar spectrum, and about magnetic fields, ring currents, auroras, the events accompanying solar flares, and the primary particles in cosmic radiation, are in the process of being solved by Soviet and American scientists with the aid of satellite-borne instruments.

The first United States IGY satellite, Explorer I, launched by the Army, was designed to measure cosmic radiation, density of meteoric matter in the satellite's orbit, and temperatures both within and on the skin of the satellite. Explorer III was also launched by the Army (Explorer II failed to orbit), and was designed to continue the measurements being made by Explorer I but with an important addition. A tiny magnetic tape recorder weighing only eight ounces enabled the satellite to store up its data for transmission to earth upon command from a designated radio receiving station in the satellite tracking network.

When Dr. James A. Van Allen and his staff at the State University of Iowa completed their preliminary analysis of the cosmic radiation data telemetered to earth by the two Explorers, they came to a startling conclusion. Although the number of cosmic rays below about 600 miles was about as expected, at greater altitudes the Geiger counters were swamped by an unexpected radiation of such intensity that they could not register it; instead they blanked out altogether.

The discovery of this intense radiation excited scientists, and instrumentation for a new IGY satellite, Explorer IV, was prepared by Dr. Van Allen and his assistants and launched by the Army in order to determine the nature and intensity of the radiation. Explorer IV carried two Geiger counters (one shielded by $\frac{1}{16}$th inch of lead) and two scintillation counters. Preliminary results indicated that the radiation is more intense and perhaps even more lethal than had been thought.

Meanwhile, other valuable data have been received from

the satellites and analyzed. The Air Force Cambridge Research Center has reported that very rough estimates by its scientists indicate that about 10,000 tons of cosmic debris are sifting onto the earth's surface every day. Nevertheless, during the lifetime of its radios, Explorer I was struck only seven or eight times by particles large enough to register.

It may be that there were no impacts on Explorer III at all. However, the possibility exists that Explorer III was damaged by a meteor shower composed of debris from the famed Halley's Comet, since its two radios failed within a day or two of each other, at 75 per cent of expected lifetime, despite separate circuitry and separate power supplies. Coincidental power failure is an unlikely explanation. On the other hand, it should be noted that Explorer I and Vanguard I continued to transmit during this period without interruption. At the moment, therefore, it does not appear that meteoric debris presents a really significant hazard to space travel.

The Jet Propulsion Laboratory of the California Institute of Technology has reported on the success of a very simple solution of space temperature problems. By covering approximately 25 per cent of the shell of the satellite with aluminum oxide stripes, temperatures within the satellite were maintained between 32°F and 104°F. This technique has therefore provided temperature control in a satellite within the range of human survival, although perhaps not comfort. With more elaborate techniques, available in a larger space vehicle, the inner temperatures could be controlled within quite narrow limits at almost any desired level.

It is said that there is no such thing as a failure in rocketry, for, with each "failure," valuable new knowledge is acquired to improve the chances of success for the next time, as well as new scientific data. Support for this statement is found in the unsuccessful Vanguard launching of May 27, 1958.

For 590 seconds after the satellite separated from the burned-out third stage, scientific data were recorded at Cape Canaveral, Florida, and Antigua, the West Indies.

Analysis of these records by scientists at the Naval Research Laboratory has led them to conclude that about 25 tons of minute meteorite particles strike the earth every day. This value is in obvious disagreement with the results reached by the Air Force Cambridge Research Center. However, the disagreement stems primarily from a difference in the method of interpreting and extrapolating the data, rather than from any difference in the observed data themselves. It is from such earnest disagreements as this that scientific facts are eventually fashioned. Undoubtedly other valuable information will also be distilled from these records.

Gradually, of course, the IGY satellite program is blending in with, and being absorbed by, the nation's continuing program for research in space. Responsibility for the nation's progress in a civilian space research and exploration program has been entrusted by the Congress to the National Aeronautics and Space Administration. Responsibility for military and defense aspects of the conquest of space remain, of course, with the Department of Defense.

In keeping with the responsibility of the National Academy of Sciences as adviser to the government on scientific problems, on August 3, 1958, Dr. Detlev W. Bronk, president of the academy, appointed a sixteen-man Space Science Board. The board, under the chairmanship of Dr. Lloyd V. Berkner, is being called upon to study scientific research opportunities and needs opened up by the advent of rocket and satellite tools; to give advice and recommendations on space science to interested agencies and institutions; to stimulate research in the rocket and satellite fields; and to cooperate in space science activities with foreign groups active in this field.

Another task before the board is to foster cooperation in the prevention of undesirable and unnecessary contamination of moon and planet surfaces and atmosphere with alien particles of energy and matter introduced from earth by space vehicles.

The academy's Space Science Board is particularly well suited to promote international cooperation in space science and to take over the present functions of the United States National Committee for IGY in this respect.

It should be remembered that the technology of space flight will probably develop gradually, so that the payloads and distances traveled will be relatively small at first, and the scientific experiments necessarily modest in the early stages. However, the Space Science Board is also giving immediate and urgent attention to proposals for more far-reaching experiments to be attempted in the very near future when more sophisticated vehicles become available.

So we stand poised near the beginning of a new era. We are preparing to enter a world which may seem strange to us but which our children will find as familiar as we found the world of motorcars. The interests of human progress and our national welfare demand that the long-term program of space exploration now being formulated be pursued by the United States with utmost energy.

Although there will inevitably be benefits of a very practical nature from such a program, the basic goal of this exploration must be the quest of knowledge about our solar system and the universe beyond. We must be prompt to seize the new opportunities for scientific observation and experiments which space technology now affords, and which will contribute so enormously to man's ultimate attainment of a better life—not only in a material or physical sense, but also intellectually and spiritually.

6.

Here is the fundamental challenge. After everything has been said about the hopes, the plans, and the machinery by which men expect to reach the planets, and perhaps eventually the stars, men still face the inescapable demand for a new outlook on their place in the universe.

For a start, we might remember that, from a cosmic viewpoint, our familiar old earth is itself a space ship. Whirling around the sun at an average speed of 18.5 miles a second, it joins the sun in circling the center of our galaxy at some 140 miles a second.

We are constantly carried on a dizzy journey through space even though, to our present limited perspective, we have stuck close to "solid earth."

The demand of the dawning space age is for men to shed this limited perspective and to acquire the cosmic viewpoint. The sun is itself a star, a very average star, and it has been estimated that there probably are at least a hundred million other planet systems that could support organic life.

In the words of the famous Harvard astronomer, Dr. Harlow Shapley, the time has come to "confront the cosmic facts squarely and fully: small but magnificent man face to face with an enormous and magnificent universe." (From *Of Stars and Men*, by Harlow Shapley, published by the Beacon Press.)

What are these "cosmic facts" as the scientists so far have uncovered them? Only a short listing can be given here.

First, there is the position of the sun and its planets in our galaxy.

According to the best astronomical assessment, the sun is a fairly average star with a long life span ahead of it. Stars like the sun are somewhat common among the 100 billion members of our Milky Way galactic system.

Most stars of this type are found out toward the edge of the system, which is flat and shaped something like a pinwheel with a central bulge (nucleus) and several spiral arms. The sun is located out in one of these spiral arms about 27,000 light years from the galactic center. (A light year is the distance light travels in a year's time. It is about 6 million million miles.)

The offside position of the sun is the reason we have the Milky Way overhead, when we are looking toward the bulk of our galaxy. Thus we see a great many more stars than when we look in other directions.

The second fact is one of numbers. The scale of the universe is unimaginably vast. The nearest star is 4 light years—that is, 24 trillion miles—away.

If the solar system were reduced to a sphere two feet in diameter, this nearest neighbor would be at a lonely distance of more than a mile. Yet it seems practically in your lap when you realize that the 200-inch Mount Palomar telescope can see several billion light years into space and that astronomers know there are more stars beyond that.

Then, too, astronomers point out that our galaxy is only one of many million such star systems within reach of their telescopes. It is conservatively estimated that these galaxies contain something like 100 million, million, million stars.

Such figures are beyond human comprehension, although it is interesting to note the dimensions of our earthly world are about halfway between the vast scale of the stellar universe and the microscale of the atom.

The third point is the probability of organic life arising throughout this vast universe.

Dr. Shapley estimates that, at the very minimum, there

are 100 million planetary systems suitable for organic life. This life might be very much like that on earth and it might be quite different. But presumably it would be characterized by intelligence, at least in some of its manifestations.

In his book, *Of Stars and Men,* Dr. Shapley asks rhetorically, "Is that biochemical operation [organic life] strangely limited to our planet, limited to No. 3 in the family of the sun, which is an average star located in the outer part of a galaxy that contains a hundred thousand million other stars—and this local galaxy but one of millions of galaxies already on the records? . . . Of course not. We are not alone."

Such are the "cosmic facts" of life in this space age. They accord to men and their planet, their star and its solar system, no special place in the universe or even within their own galaxy.

At first sight and from a limited human viewpoint, these "cosmic facts" are overwhelmingly humbling. They seem to relegate humanity to almost total insignificance. But, again to quote Dr. Shapley, there is "nothing very humiliating about our material inconsequentiality."

"Are we debased," he asks, "by the greater speed of the sparrow, the larger size of the hippopotamus, the keener hearing of the dog? . . . We should also take the stars in our stride."

Certainly there is nothing inconsequential about men who can compass the universe with concept and thought. And the demand of the space age is that they do just that.

Scientists have been facing this demand for many years. What do they think it implies in the way of a new outlook? Here is a consensus abstracted from the many discussions they have held on the subject.

First, they believe it is abundantly evident that the human race can no longer consider itself unique. The high probability of other intelligent races on other worlds, the very sweep of cosmic immensity as it appears through the telescopes, show that mankind's real challenge in space flight is to find its proper place in the universe.

As a practical consequence, American space scientists generally urge the formulation of a long-range nonmilitary research program of high priority. And beyond that they urge that all possible effort be extended to put space exploration under international auspices.

They recognize that the military and political circumstances of present times demand an alert defense policy in regard to military uses of space. But they are also convinced that men will be deluding themselves if they do not look beyond the limited horizon of weapons development.

Mankind is not entering space as a conquering hero, they say. It is, rather, in the position of an adolescent youngster being let out on his own for the first time. Its real challenge and opportunity is to discover the great outside world and make its own adjustments to the realities.

This calls for an attitude of humble exploration rather than of strident conquest and that attitude needs to be adopted right now as the first plans for space flight are being formulated.

The second conclusion of the scientists is that, in entering space, men cannot turn their backs on the earth. The scientific and technical achievements that are making this possible must first be applied to enriching the life of men on their own planet, if the great adventure in confronting the cosmos is to pay its full dividends.

The corollary of the conclusion that mankind is not unique in the universe is that all men are brothers. The divisions of earthbound humanity have no more significance in the cosmic equation than does the ordinary family quarrel in the political economy of earth.

Translated into practical terms, this implies that, if men are to get anywhere in space, they must in the long run work together. But that kind of cooperation over the decades and centuries of the future requires that it first be worked out in tackling common problems on earth.

Such then are the broad implications arising from the new perspective evoked by mankind's entry into space.

"It is a magnificent universe in which to play a part, however humble," says Dr. Shapley. The challenge of space flight is the opportunity it offers men to find out how magnificent that "humble" part may actually be.

The assault on space will require broad-gauge thinking. It will be an antidote for pettiness. And it can absorb all the excess energies, inventiveness, resources, and derring-do which mankind has on tap.

It represents perhaps the point at which invention reaches closest to—and is most inspired by—that limitless infinity which the cosmic universe dimly shadows forth.

AWAKENING OF PEOPLES

Abdul Listens to Tomorrow

1.

SOMEWHERE HIS NAME IS ABDUL. WHILE WE PONDER A FLIGHT to the stars, he worries about a road to the village. He is bound now by ignorance or poverty or politics. But he is listening to tomorrow. And for his sake, and ours, we must listen too.

For he is in the majority. He wants, and he is slowly getting, the things we take for granted—food, learning, self-government, progress.

What does he hear as he listens to his beckoning future?

We can't ask him as a faceless member of the mass. We must go to his hut or his paddy or his farm. He may disagree with his neighbor—or, like Sakharam Powar in India, with his son. . . .

Sakharam scooped up a tiny clod of earth, looked at it, kissed it, and lovingly crumbled it through his fingers back into the dust. Then his eyes swept the translucent bowl above for the first signs of the black, pot-bellied rain clouds which would end the long torment of summer.

Every hot-weather dawn for the last thirty years has seen Sakharam Powar perform the same little ceremony as he arrives on his stamp-sized fields in a fold of the Sivalik Hills of western India. And every dusk finds him repeating the actions of his forefathers as he plows, sows, and reaps according to a rigid traditional pattern.

Two fields away, within back-chatting distance, and similarly employed, is son Dhondu. But there ends the similarity. For bare-bodied Sakharam, burned black by the searing flame of thirty summers, is the very symbol of ageless, unchanging, never-ending Hindustan—hard and gnarled as a piece of hickory, magnificent in his confidence of wresting a living with his bare hands, exasperating in his know-all obstinacy, his resistance to change. Whereas Dhondu, in ragged T shirt and faded jeans, while equally obstinate, is quickening to change, impatient to supplement the skill of his hands, scornful of everything Sakharam holds dear. He is the very essence of rebellion.

Between the two a fierce rivalry has sprung up. It all began a dozen years ago when, on the crests of the surrounding hills, bonfires blazed the news of Indian independence. On this night in August, peace left a quiet Indian homestead. Dhondu, neglecting his fields, took a holiday and spent the night dancing in the village square. "Ai [mother], who rushed through her chores to hang garlands of marigold and frangipani all over the thatch hut, wore sprays of scented jasmine in her hair, like a young bride," grumbled Sakharam.

In the following ten years, Dhondu grew to manhood and, responding to the atmosphere, began to disobey his father with increasing frequency and apply new methods to the field which Sakharam had given him. He borrowed money to buy bags of fertilizer and seed. He began to plow differently, following the contours of his land. In a part of the field, he sowed rice, as in Japan, and found that this method yielded a bumper crop. He persuaded Ai to keep poultry, and in his spare time helped her clear the back yard in order to grow vegetables. Sakharam, meanwhile, simmered like a near-active volcano. Willingly dependent on the monsoons for his water, he raised only a single rice crop a year and in the intervening dry season was content to hire himself out as a daily wage laborer.

Dhondu repudiated this happy-go-lucky attitude. He planned to dig irrigation ditches, work with other villagers on a feeder canal, and so grow two crops a year. As a result, discord erupted at home. Then Ai, crouching over her cooking pots, surreptitiously wiped her eyes with the ragged end of her sari. For torn between the old and the new, she remains wife and mother, loving her husband, admiring her son, and less and less able to reconcile the two emotions.

Every evening the battle is renewed. "Independence," scoffs Sakharam, "only makes us more and more dependent on others. In my father's time, we needed nothing outside our village. Now Dhondu has to read out of a book before he sows." Dhondu retaliates by throwing in his father's face his last year's bumper crop and challenges him to do as well this year.

This is a part of the story of India today, a story of tension and upheaval, of breaking homes and last-ditch stands, of a resurgence of youth and womanhood. It is a story of the dwindling prestige of wealth and of a caste system which is loosening its iron bands. It is a story of the overthrow of the citadels of orthodoxy.

Gandhi's gentle breeze of freedom has grown into a wayward wind which, blowing this way and that, is sweeping away both the bad and the good in the established order. Gone is the respect for age and tradition which has kept this nation quiescent for a thousand years. Gone also is its surface serenity and courage, which apathy bred. Suffering no longer is a badge of pride, but of unnecessary ignorance. On August

15, 1947, as Imperial Britain proudly marched out with all its banners flying, there ended one great revolution and began a much greater one. India's 400 million awoke to the ferment of progress.

Sakharam's family is not the only one that has been sundered. At New Delhi, far from Sakharam's humble field, is the marble rotunda where sits the House of the People, India's lower house. There five hundred elected members of Parliament have front seats at a family drama, which daily enacted reminds them of the tremendous changes which they are helping bring about in this nation's social order.

Just behind the treasury benches on the speaker's right hand sits a soft-spoken, home-spun-draped legislator, who once was a minister in his home state of Madras and now is a parliamentary stalwart of the ruling Congress party. Slightly left of center sits his son, a prominent member of the Peoples' Socialist party, and, a few benches away, farther to the left but as far removed ideologically as the North Pole, is the daughter. She adorns the benches of the Communist party of India. And it is not uncommon for the House to remain in uncomfortable silence while the members of this Indian family fiercely dispute a point and suggest widely differing solutions.

Not so long ago, these three lived together, worked together in the freedom movement, and were members of a single political organization. Now, after a dozen years of independence, fierce antagonisms mar friendship and civil war rages where once there was harmony of purpose.

The Hindu joint family was an institution which survived centuries of invasions. As a clan, close-knit and impervious to change, it kept alive in itself the intrinsic oneness of the country even when Indian entity was no more than a geographic expression.

But now it is faltering under political and economic pressures. The father is less the lord and master of the home than once he was, the mother no longer the stern matriarch who directed and influenced every life and who used the daughter-in-law as a domestic drudge.

For, apart from politics, the changing pattern of economy has forced the children to leave home in search of employment. In their new environment they pick up new friends, adapt themselves to new customs, intermingle with new communities, imbibe new ideas, and put their hand to all kinds of new work.

Consequently, with the Hindu joint family now no longer a single unit, there is seen the breaking up of the caste system. Two generations ago for a Hindu to marry outside his caste was considered bad; for him to marry a Moslem made him an outcast. A union between a Brahmin—the highest caste—with the Harijan (Untouchable) led to riots, with the bride and groom and their usually unhappy families having to be protected from the wrath of their respective communities.

In the villages this still is the order of the day, but in the towns and cities, to which more and more villagers flock each year, caste has lost its sanctity.

In recent times, with taxes no longer being computed with the Hindu family as a unit, the trends toward freedom from parental and family control have been vastly accelerated.

And when, two years ago, Parliament decreed that the Hindu wife could divorce her husband and the Hindu daughter inherit her father's wealth, the whole fabric of Indian society began to disintegrate.

This disintegration now is the subject of a nationwide controversy. On the side of quick progress by forced marches are the government, Parliament, India's youth, and the leaders of its emancipation movements. In the opposite camp are still powerful Hindu orthodoxy, a substantial segment of the upper and middle classes, the village hierarchy, and, strangely enough, many social workers who feel that, since the nation always has been rooted in the family, the rapid dissolution of the latter is causing much confusion and unhappiness in this interim period.

These workers are right when they maintain that the changes in India are too sweeping to be contained in the decade in which they were made. Thousands of slumbering villages, awakened by change, are in ferment. In these villages wealth has lost its meaning, traditions of caste and community unceremoniously flung into a melting pot. In the towns and cities, a bustling new generation tramples on measured progress and hustles forward to adopt the modes and manners of the Western world.

Is it any surprise, therefore, that on the faces of most Indians these days there is a look of bewilderment? Something tremendous is happening, only no one is very sure what it is and whether it is good or bad. Everything that was on top is at the bottom; not everything at the bottom has got to the top. Freedom, that great leveler, has come to a country where once privilege ruled.

It is a mighty wind which has blown maharajas off their gorgeously caparisoned elephants and great feudal lords from their estates. It has blown village schoolmasters into seats of high authority and untouchables into the innermost sanctums of the most holy Hindu shrines. The hot Indian sun still shines, but no one can slumber in its rays.

2.

Elsewhere in Asia an analysis of the future is complicated by the mingling of races. For example, in Malaya almost any three people you meet are likely to be of different races. Abdul is a farmer, Tung Foo a tin miner, Mutu a rubber tapper. Racially they are Malay, Chinese, and Indian respectively.

The culmination of change and progress for them since the end of World War II is the current requirement that they appreciate themselves and one another now as Malayans, as equal citizens of the federation which became one of the world's newest independent nations August 31, 1957.

It takes a bit of doing, as the British say. The inherited customs and outlook of the three differ widely as they share the responsibility conferred upon a multiracial population by the departure of the British from the administrative controls.

Unlike the inhabitants of some emancipated countries, Abdul, Tung Foo, Mutu, and all the rest of the federation's 6.5 million people have come to their collective independence without having to fight for it. Indeed, they did not particularly see it. Indigenous leaders secured it for them without rousing passion. The British helped these leaders to find it far quicker than ever expected. Now the leaders are learning administration by experience.

What has this meant in terms of change to Abdul, the farmer? Well, for one thing, a call to quicken the tempo of life, to listen more to what he is told by the Rural and Industrial Development Authority, to strengthen the cooperatives which can help him, as well as the country's fishermen, to cut out the middleman who has exploited him in the past. The number of such cooperatives has grown since World War II to 2,300, of forty-two different types, with a working capital equivalent to nearly 17 million American dollars.

Abdul, however, is conservative. His general idea in the past has been to raise enough rice or whatever else for family needs and only a little more for kampong (village) luxuries. As a consequence the Malays, 60 per cent of whom live by agriculture, have economically fallen behind the second and third largest racial communities in Malaya—the Chinese and the Indians.

The government's effort now is to persuade the Malays to catch up and to help them to do so—by irrigation, electric power, and other schemes affecting large numbers and by introducing means for increased productive and distributive efficiency to the individual. Abdul has not always been so responsive as was hoped. But he is coming along.

Tung Foo is a different sort of person. Happily not one of the ten thousand miners laid off in 1958 owing to the depressive effect on production of international price control for tin, he has been operating with the characteristic assid[uity] of his race in Malaya.

The Chinese are less than a million fewer than the Malays and they work like beavers—mostly in every sort of urban commercial enterprise, big and small. Originally they came to mine tin, of which the federation produces almost one-third of the world's supply, as it does of natural rubber.

Communally the Chinese have lived for themselves and were encouraged to do so by a British policy protective of Malays as the indigenous occupants of the land. Integration with the Malays, following the exit of the British, calls for reciprocal confidence in the reconciliation of differing interests.

And what about Mutu, the rubber tapper? The great change of his life since World War II—and it has affected many other types of Malayan workers as well—is the enormously increased protective power of his trade union. Collective bargaining power, with the ready threat of striking, has raised wages and kept them up. Living conditions in the labor lines have been improved.

From southern India, Mutu has a political bent. It put him on the road to communism at one time—until an ugly instance of terrorism by jungle gunmen on the estate where he works frightened him into reverse. Armed Communists, nine out of every ten of whom are Chinese, have tried since 1948 to impose their will from the jungles covering four-fifths of Malaya. There are still thirteen hundred gunmen there, but they are now far less dangerous to Mutu, Abdul, and Tung Foo than the Communists operating unarmed and slyly outside the jungle.

The great demand of our three friends' new freedom upon them is that they defend it by collective awareness as the nation they are building now takes shape.

In Singapore, which became internally self-governing in 1959, the future holds new promise and problems, particularly for young Chinese like Ah Too. To this little girl and her family the changes which have led up to that situation since the end of World War II, particularly since a mainly elected government took office in 1955, will seem slight compared with those ahead.

For Chinese-speaking Chinese and China-born Chinese have acquired for the first time the same rights and privileges as all other citizens in Singapore.

Ah Too will go to a school in a Chinese educational system for which more has been done since the middle 1950's than in all the previous time since Sir Stamford Raffles put the British flag over this strategic little Malayan island in 1819.

Ah Too is a symbol of youth in a state where, by 1965,

nearly half of 2 million inhabitants (80 per cent Chinese) will be children fourteen years old or less. Forty-six per cent is the precise estimate.

Every eight minutes another Singaporean is born. Hence the perpetual crowd scene in those narrow streets where family washing, thrust out of upper windows on poles, vies for brightness with the colored characters of Chinese shop signs below. New roads and more and more building show that the challenge of congestion is being answered, though not fast enough.

Already, with the average wage rate risen by 12 per cent since 1954, 10 per cent of the population (1.5 million now) are living in homes built with government subsidy for rents that go as low as 20 local dollars (less than 7 American) a month.

In the more spacious residential areas, old houses with extensive grounds are being pulled down to provide space for many small homes.

When Ah Too's father was asked what he thought were the greatest changes in the life of Singapore's Chinese since he was at school twelve years ago, he said, "More done for the people, more money—and politics."

Politics were introduced on party lines for general elections as recently as 1955. They represent the most spectacular postwar addition to the life of a cosmopolitan public including Chinese, Malays, Indians, Pakistanis, Ceylonese, British, and others. The Communist party is banned and works surreptitiously, infiltrating the People's Action party (PAP), on the left of the legitimate political line, as well as social institutions, particularly schools, though these are less vulnerable now that the educational system has been reorganized.

So Ah Too's father is being urged to join the new United Socialist Front, in process of launching by Singapore's Chief

Minister, Lim Yew Hock. Most of her father's friends, however, are in the PAP, which counsels otherwise. He, like Singapore itself, is at the political crossroads, whether he wants to be or not.

3.

Asians everywhere, indeed, are having to make up their minds. Future challenges for peoples advancing toward self-government may be previewed in the present experience of Kintaro Yanagizawa and Ichiro Kimura of Japan.

Democracy as an American postwar export commodity means different things to different people in the tightly packed and fast-moving island home of some 90-odd million Japanese.

For some it has been a full awakening to the benefits which derive from the calculated practice of modern, democratic freedoms. For others, the process has been slower, chiefly because, as in most Asian states, it takes time for new ideas to penetrate from the big cities to the traditionally more conservative rural areas.

The case of Kintaro Yanagizawa, who grows apples high up in one of the valleys which separate the Japan Alps, falls in the second category. Yanagizawa-san and his family are tasting, so to speak, the fruits of Japan's democratic conversion, though they have not yet entered into the stage wherein there is a conscious practice of its precepts.

Being the eldest son, Yanagizawa automatically inherited the family homestead, and, as is normally the case, the second and third sons went to the cities to scratch out a living in other fields.

Yanagizawa-san was too young to go to war, but he was old enough to understand that wartime life in the village of Maruko in Nagano Prefecture was one of constant restrictions, tight surveillance, and extreme hardship. The bonds were suddenly cut in 1945, and, in the hiatus which followed defeat, he decided to give up the time-worn art of nurturing the silkworm on the mulberry tree, and lay out an orchard consisting of some seventy apple trees.

This was Yanagizawa-san's first experience in postwar freedom. And, although the going was at times difficult, he stuck by his trees, laying out a half acre of rice as a cash crop when frost, insects, or prices cut into his apple crop proceeds.

General of the Army Douglas MacArthur's land-reform program divided up the township's biggest farm estate. And while Yanagizawa and his neighbors did not fully comprehend the theory behind land reforms, they understood that in their case it created more independent operators, gave each operator a greater sense of personal dignity, and removed semifeudal impediments to the flow of free bank credits.

Today, Yanagizawa has not much to say about democracy. But he understands that it has contributed to his own personal welfare.

There was a bumper crop in 1957, thanks to the availability of chemical fertilizers and insecticides with which Yanagizawa sprays his crop some fifteen times during the growing season.

Free travel has made it possible for the township's cooperative to import workers from northern Honshu to wrap each apple in paper during frost season, and to help in the picking. And the cooperative itself, operating along democratic lines, buys Yanagizawa-san's crop, boxes it, ships it to port centers, and takes part in export to many parts of the world.

In 1957, reflecting the improved living standard of Japanese farmers, Yanagizawa-san made enough net profit to buy

a three-wheeled truck. Besides this, he had enough left over
to take his wife and two children occasionally to a neighboring hot-spring resort, and to go into near-by Ueda city once a
week for his preference in entertainment—American movies.
Tough-muscled and sunburned, Yanagizawa has achieved
a new level of dignity. But not all the old habits have
sloughed off. When his daughter grows up, he will insist upon
the traditional arranged marriage, as was the case with his
sister Sumiko. And if he has more than two sons, the oldest
will get the farm, even though the land-reform program speci-
fies equal division among sons.

Sitting beside his charcoal brazier after a day in the
orchard, Yanagizawa-san peels a hot sweet potato and phi-
losophizes much like Japan's other 18 million farmers:

"We do not understand much about democracy, but if it
means that we can continue to earn a living according to our
own choice and without any restrictions, then we are for it."

While democracy is not yet a conscious way of life for
Yanagizawa-san, it is for Ichiro Kimura, a still youthful
barber who owns and runs a small shop in back of Tokyo's
central Nihonbashi district.

When Japan went to war, Kimura-san was drafted. He was
sent with the Japanese Imperial expeditionary forces to China
and saw, but did not take part in, action at Nanking. Kimura-
san was the battalion haircutter.

After surrender in 1945, Kimura-san was repatriated in an
American LST from Shanghai. He returned to find that his
home had been burned. Worse than that, there seemed no
opportunity for him to set up a shop for himself.

Some friends suggested that he apply to the United States
occupation forces for a job. He did this, and got a job as a
greaser in a downtown Tokyo motor pool.

The sergeant in charge of the motor pool discovered, after

some time, that Kimura-san was acquainted with the art of haircutting, and he was promptly elevated to the post of company barber.

From there Kimura-san gravitated to the Dai Iti Hotel basement, where field-grade United States officers came to the hotel barber shop and left behind relatively lavish tips.

By the time of the peace treaty in 1951, Kimura-san had accumulated sufficient capital to buy three used barber chairs and set up his own shop in rented premises.

"But I was not satisfied to be just a barber," he explains, pointing to a pile of books on the shelf over his washstand. "In Japan we no longer have to stay in a certain bracket; we are free to move upward in the professional scale, so I am going to night school to study electrical engineering," he added proudly.

Like most urban Japanese, Kimura-san keeps a pretty tight schedule. Each morning he gets up shortly after sunrise—4:30 A.M. in the summer. After a breakfast of cold rice, a bit of fish, and dried seaweed, he races for the electric train and, after standing in a queue for ten or fifteen minutes, muscles himself into the tightly packed train. He does a part of his homework hanging onto the strap before he is dumped out at Nihonbashi station.

"Democracy has brought us many things, but not enough trains and buses," he ruefully remarks. Someone else observed that crowded Tokyo manages to exist only because a good one-third of the more than 8 million population is riding the trains at one time or another during the day.

Kimura-san takes a break at noontime when a boy brings in a bowl of noodles. Then at six-thirty he locks the shop door and races off to night school.

He gets home at about eleven and his wife, whom he

chose himself contrary to past custom, sits up while he eats another meal of cold rice and fish. This is the schedule for six out of seven days a week.

On Sundays, Kimura-san, his wife, and young son take a holiday. Again Kimura-san wrestles with the trains and buses, and, along with a few thousand other Japanese, is dumped out at some stop in the "country" a few miles outside the city limits. While his wife and child play and read Japanese comic books, Kimura-san studies wiring blueprints for his Monday night class.

"Certainly, we live in a two-room house and share the kitchen," he explains, adding, "but nobody interferes with our lives as they did during the war and before." He concludes:

"Today, a Japanese can make anything of himself that he wants—it just takes hard work. I can vote as I please, and my wife can speak her piece before the Women's Association. I know nothing about Marx, and very little about your President Eisenhower. But for us Japanese, democracy is a great thing."

Certain elements of democracy, however, are too much of a great thing for some Japanese, like the irate accountant who wrote to the editor of one of Tokyo's leading dailies: "It is an outrage that Japanese women should be permitted to shoulder their way into crowded trains, grab seats for themselves, and leave us men standing."

Admittedly, the writer was a bit behind the times, and probably never had read any of the national laws of Japan governing the new status of women.

When United States occupation troops first tramped up the dusty road from Yokohama to Tokyo in 1945, the average Japanese woman was little more than a graceful and efficient ornament of home and society. She dutifully walked three paces behind her husband in public, ate her meals separately, bowed to the dictums of the head of the family, and stood aside when family properties and estates were doled out to her exclusion.

Today, particularly in the urban centers, there has been a noticeable change. The flowing Japanese kimono is disappearing. And with it, the "democratized" Japanese woman is beginning to take part in the family councils. She joins housewife associations that pressure the government on legislation affecting households, and, as the mounting national divorce rate testifies, she exercises her legal prerogatives when other means fail.

Arranged marriages are becoming rare in the big cities, though the custom still prevails in rural areas. Japanese women frequently go into business for themselves. And the fact that eleven women were elected to the House of Representatives in the May, 1958, election testifies to the fact that they enjoy a small but significant niche in the top echelons of Japan's political hierarchy.

Women in Tokyo alone make up one-third of the workers, one-fifth of the university students, and a significant share of the various government bureaus up to the rank of bureau chief.

Naturally, the new freedoms have brought excesses. Older Japanese, for instance, complain there is a tendency toward *dasan teki* or the selfish attitude—"get what you can while you can." But this might be the expected result of any social revolution in which old systems are disappearing and new ones erected empirically.

Like any social innovation, however, the new status for women of Japan is slower to take hold in the rural areas than it is in the cities.

A recent government survey, for instance, shows that in 93

per cent of Japan's 6 million farm families, the husband makes all the decisions whether it be the menu or whom to vote for in an election.

While city girls now generally pick their own husbands, the country girl—or at least an estimated 52 per cent of them —prefer to have their fathers pick a spouse.

One might call it equality when the farm women work in icy water along with the men planting rice ten hours a day. But when the day is over, it is over only for the men. While the men bathe and sit about the charcoal brazier reading the papers, the womenfolk have to prepare meals, serve them, eat their own alone, and then clear up afterward —which may not sound wholly unfamiliar to a working woman in any country.

When a farm household discovers that the family budget will not support an extra daughter, she is shuffled off to one of the near-by cities to work in a factory, as a housemaid, or as a clerk in a department store.

She may live in a company dormitory or, if she is fortunate, in a four-by-six-foot rented room. But she quickly learns independence. She manages her own budget, chooses her own friends, comes and goes as she pleases, and, if she is thrifty, gets a new dress once a year.

When it comes time for her to return to the homestead, she has learned many things which rural Japan could not teach her. She may dutifully submit to an arranged marriage. But she is unlikely, once having tasted freedom, to submit gracefully to the old role.

4.

Thus the story of the awakening of peoples always comes back to the individual. Moving from the Far East to the Middle East, that story might focus on Moshe Levin at the

Kibbutz Netzer-Sereni in Israel. How is Moshe forging his
future?

Moshe Levin is a well-built man in his mid-thirties. It is
difficult to believe that he weighed 75 pounds when Negro
troops of the United States Eighth Army freed him from a
concentration camp at Garmisch-Partenkirchen, Germany,
in 1945.

In the tiny office in the corner of the small kibbutz (collective) factory, Mr. Levin is hunched over a table spread
with blueprints. He is working on plans trying to improve
the bodies of 34-ton trailers his factory is building. The
trailers are used to transport raw materials from the Negev
to Israel's industrial centers.

Watching his concentration, one hardly would think that
the future of this quiet, smiling man was shaped by a series
of wars, revolutions, underground fighting, persecutions, and
tortures on two continents.

As a boy of sixteen, he watched Soviet tanks roll through
the streets of his native Kowno, capital of Lithuania—termi-
nating orderly life for him, his brothers, sisters, parents, and
most of his friends and acquaintances. His father's shop and
property were confiscated, and he soon had to leave school
as a son of a "capitalist exploiter."

Hitler's armies drove the Soviets from Kowno the next year.
Caught between hammer and anvil, Moshe tried to escape
in the direction of Smolensk, but was captured and brought
back by the Germans to the new Jewish ghetto there.

Four years of existence in concentration camps followed.
Forced labor and starvation, escape and partisan fighting, re-
capture and new persecutions marked his life.

"I never was a Zionist," Mr. Levin explains. "As a child in
Kowno, I dreamed of becoming an interior decorator and

sometimes thought I would emigrate to the United States, which I heard was a land of limitless scope.

"But life changed all this," he went on. "I was tortured and humiliated as a Jew, and the majority of my friends and family were killed because they were Jews. So I decided this should never happen again." He pounded his clenched fist on the table to emphasize the point he made. On his arm, one read the tattooed number 87768—a "souvenir" of the Dachau concentration camp.

"I decided to go to Palestine where I heard Jews were trying to build a new homeland," he said.

He received an immigration certificate under the limited quota which the British mandate administration issued beginning in 1946, and landed in Haifa soon after. But he found no peace in the strife-torn Holy Land. This was the twilight of British rule in Palestine, marked by disorders and bloodshed.

He had been working for a calm and settled life, so he joined a collective settlement, Kibbutz Givat Brenner, as soon as he arrived. But shortly afterward, he was caught up in the movement which organized an "underground railway" for Jewish refugees from Europe, most of whom the British excluded from the Holy Land.

On moonless nights, he helped to unload the human cargoes of the small illegal vessels. When the British rounded up members of the illegal Jewish defense organization in June, 1946, Moshe, too, was arrested. Once again, he was behind barbed wire. This time, he was guarded by the British.

After three months he was released and resumed activities in the underground. Then, when the State of Israel was proclaimed in 1948, the underground was transformed into Israel's regular army, and Moshe was given the three bars of a captain. He fought in the Judean Hills around Jeru-

salem, in Galilee, and in Operation Ten Plagues, which led
to the collapse of the Egyptian forces.

He left the army as soon as the war ended. He went back
to Givat Brenner and married Rachel, an attractive teacher,
born in the same kibbutz. A few months later, they left the
well-established, old kibbutz of Givat Brenner and helped
to develop a new collective settlement near by, that of
Netzer-Sereni.

Here he showed skill in handling complex machinery in
the mechanical workshop of the kibbutz. During the day he
helped to repair tools, and in the evenings he read and
studied books on mechanical engineering. The kibbutz recognized his aptitude and sent him for a year's course to the
Israel Institute of Technology in Haifa. Today, he is technical
manager of the kibbutz mechanical factory supervising the
work of fifty member workers.

Six days a week Mr. Levin gets up at 6:30 A.M., and after
a shower, shaves with a Soviet-made electric razor—a gift
from a new immigrant from Poland. He goes to the communal dining hall for breakfast consisting of cottage cheese,
an egg, margarine, olives, tomatoes, cucumbers, jam, and
bread.

At 7:15 A.M. he is in the factory and works eight hours a
day, with about a two-hour break at noon. He meets his wife
in the communal dining hall. She comes in from the kibbutz
school. Lunch is the main meal and consists of soup, meat or
fish, vegetables, salad, and fruit or cakes.

After the work ends at 5 P.M., he walks to his living
quarters near by. By the time he has taken a shower, his
wife is also home. So are their three sons, ranging between
one and five years of age. The youngest son is brought in
from the communal nursery, while the other two come from
the kindergarten of the kibbutz.

After dinner, Moshe and Rachel usually divide their time between the children, reading (for Moshe this means mainly technical literature) and recreation. In the kibbutz recreation consists of lectures, concerts, and movies in the same communal hall.

Like other members of the kibbutz, Moshe receives no salary. Earnings of the kibbutz go to the communal treasury, out of which all members are fed, clothed, housed, and financed in their cultural and recreational needs.

Moshe takes the visitor to his small house some 300 yards from his factory. His wife is attending a teachers' conference in a near-by immigrants' village. One looks at the two neat rooms, small hall, and bathroom—all furnished simply but in good taste (part of the furniture made by Moshe).

"Do I feel happy?" Moshe repeats the question. "There are no limits to man's desires. Personally, I have everything I need. But I would like, of course, to expand our factory."

He brings out a neatly bound album of his children's photos. "Look at them," he says with shining eyes. "They are happy. I only hope they will have a calm and free life and will never taste the bitter experiences of persecution."

5.

On the other side of a tragic boundary, separated by more than miles from Mr. Levin's kibbutz, a young Arab intellectual in Egypt answers the questions of a Western friend:

Q.: Why are most university graduates and undergraduates of our generation in the Arab world angry young men?

A.: Not angry young men, but crusaders.

Q.: Crusaders for what?

A.: Crusaders to make the rest of the world treat us as equals, and to establish a greater measure of social justice here in the Middle East.

Q.: That's fine. But a lot of people feel that you're always crusading against somebody or something instead of for some positive ideal. Most of the Arab countries of the Middle East are now sovereign and independent, and we get a bit tired of your lectures about Western imperialism.

A.: You miss the point. The West is still not reconciled to letting us stand on our own feet, to letting us go the way of our own choosing. The West still thinks that it can use the Sixth Fleet or economic sanctions to bend us to its will. Arab nationalism existed long before Nasser, but why do you think most Arab nationalists have made Nasser their hero and champion? Because Nasser is the first Arab leader who has had the strength and the skill to stand up to the West and get away with it. He has shown the West that it can no longer humiliate us with impunity.

Q.: But why are all your suspicions concentrated against the West? Doesn't the Soviet Union have its own brutal brand of imperialism?

A.: Look, who threatens us most immediately and directly? The West or the Soviet Union? Who bombed Cairo and invaded Egypt at the time of the Suez crisis? Who keeps a battle fleet just below the horizon whenever there is an internal crisis in Jordan, Syria, or Lebanon? Who keeps military bases in the Arab world largely against the wishes of the people of the countries where the bases are? Who has been trying for the past two years to undermine the position of Nasser, the standard bearer of contemporary Arab nationalism? And whatever the sins of the Soviet Union, you cannot deny that in our moments of greatest need it has repeatedly come forward with valuable diplomatic support.

Q.: Wait a moment. Don't forget that the United States took a stand for morality at the time of Suez, and in effect sided with Nasser and the Arabs, even at the risk of a break with its traditional allies, Britain and France.

A.: Yes, but what really happened? There was talk of economic sanctions to punish those whom the United Nations had condemned as aggressors. Who got punished in the end? Egypt, the victim of the aggression. Egyptian dollar holdings in the United States were frozen and were kept frozen for eighteen months. Point Four aid to Egypt was stopped. There was no such delay in resuming American aid to Israel.

Q.: Why were so many Arabs reluctant to join in censuring the Soviet Union for its ruthless repression of the Hungarian revolt?

A.: First of all, you must understand that we are tired of being pressured by the West in an attempt to get us to take sides in the cold war. We feel we have our own problems nearer home, problems in which we find the West against us. You are being rather naïve if you expected the Arabs at the height of the emotions stirred by the Suez crisis to have time even to think about Hungary. I will admit that many of us, even those with leftist leanings, were badly shaken this year by the execution of former Hungarian Premier Nagy and his colleagues. But because of the support which the Soviet Union gave to the Arab nationalist cause at the time of Suez and the Hungarian rising, we prefer to keep our thoughts to ourselves.

Don't think that we are basically pro-Soviet. We don't want to be committed to either of the two great power blocs. If we have affinities with any body, it is with you in the West, not with the Russians. Yet why do you continually affront us and rebuff us? We got our ideas of nationalism from you. We got our ideas of social justice from you. Many of us have tremendous admiration for British parliamentary democracy and American technical achievements. And yet when you

come to deal with us, we feel terribly disillusioned. Think of
the hopes raised by Roosevelt's idealism and the Atlantic
Charter. But now that the Americans are involved in the
Middle East, we find them naïve and arrogant—and we can't
forget the part they played in forcing on us the great injustice
of the State of Israel. We thought, too, that the British Labor
party would revolutionize the British approach to the Middle
East, but their people who've come out here have been irri-
tatingly condescending and didactic. And not only they. So
many of you from the West seem to forget that we are human
beings who react to politeness—or more important, the lack
of it—just like yourselves.

Q.: Why do you—and other Arab nationalists—accept the
authoritarian aspects of Nasser's rule?

A.: You have a point there. For some of us it has meant a
crise de conscience. But we have watched Nasser, and we
trust his intentions. His revolution was not a bloody one; and
despite his military background, his handling of domestic
affairs is neither brutal nor ruthless. Another important thing
is that he has kept himself individually free from the slightest
taint of corruption. You must understand, too, that Nasser has
effectively identified himself with social reform, which all of
us believe is an essential prerequisite to the building of a
healthy society in the Arab world. There must be a greater
sharing of wealth and a narrowing of the great gap between
the few fantastically rich and the millions of pitiably poor.

Nasser has fired imaginations throughout this area by doing
something about this in his own country. And don't forget
that the West has made things much more difficult for itself
in the Arab world by continuing to identify itself with those
forces—in Saudi Arabia, the Persian Gulf, Iraq, and Jordan—
whose hitherto privileged position would be undermined by
any revolutionary change for the better in the social order.

Q.: What about the future? Are you optimistic?
A.: If we were not, there would be no point in trying, would there?

6.

Farther south and west in the exploding continent of Africa, another young man listens to the future. His name is Henry. His country is Ghana.

"Free-DOM" is the word Ghana knows best.

Babies are christened with it, buses named affectionately after it, and it is emblazoned across enough dress material in Accra's stores to last the women of the city for many anniversaries to come.

At 1957's independence celebrations, crowds chanted it through night after night, accenting the last syllable heavily like all Ghanaians. A year and a half later, Henry rolls it thoughtfully around his tongue and starts to explain its impact upon his country.

Saxophones sob in the background, for Henry always entertains his visitors at one of Accra's simple cafés—a few chairs scattered around a slab of concrete dance floor, while an exuberant band pounds out the jazzy, calypso-style rhythms which capture all the youthful dash and energy and color of Ghana today. The cafés are cheap, and the fact is that eighteen months of freedom had not brought the prices at Accra's sole swank hotel, the Ambassador, within the reach of a university student like Henry nor of many other Ghanaians.

Indeed, independence has not brought sudden wealth, nor fulfilled any of the wilder material hopes which some less sophisticated Ghanaians entertained at the time when Britain relinquished control.

The police force, for example, has not been abolished, as

a colorful market "mammy," or trader, assured one it soon
would be.

The government has not shared out the reserve funds of
the Cocoa Marketing Board which, as one Accra man worked
out painstakingly, about the time of independence, would
mean a bonus to each citizen of £1,453 or $4,068.40.

Nor have the rattling, crowded "mammy wagons," or
trucks, been replaced with the purring American limousines
which some Ghanaians believed self-government would
somehow bring them.

"Free-DOM," in short, has not turned Ghana into a fairy-
land of Cadillac coaches and gingerbread houses. To many,
it has not brought even the good, solid down-to-earth houses
for which there is a serious need.

Fortunately, many Ghanaians, like Henry, had more en-
lightened expectations. And neither the bored English accent, which he has copied from his tutors at the University
College of Ghana, nor the spectacles which he does not need
but which, like many Africans, he perches on his broad black
nose to give him a more scholarly air, can disguise the excitement and pride which grips him at being part of Ghana's
pioneering experiment in African self-government.

For if the bulk of Ghana's 5 million people are mainly concerned with internal affairs, the politicians and intellectuals
like Henry are deeply conscious of the fact that they are in
the van of Africa's explosive emergence, that they are in the
forefront of a movement destined to win for the black African
an influential place in world affairs.

It is all a heady business for these excited young men in
brilliantly colored togas and sandals, the traditional dress
of Ghana. Since the coming of independence they have been
subjected to a constant stream of newspapermen and observers using Ghana as a yardstick in an attempt to evaluate

the prospects of Africans achieving stable government in successive colonies to be freed.

Some government actions have jolted the complacency of these earnest young students, some of them only recently from primitive backgrounds, who now are steeping themselves in the philosophies of Jefferson and Lincoln and tracing the history of political liberalism in Europe in their lecture rooms up on Accra's Legion Hill.

There has been much debate over the government's deportation of various opposition political leaders, its barring of certain newsmen, some of its "tough" legislation, and the threatening speeches of some of its Cabinet ministers.

Yet these restrictions are beginning to drive home to the people of Ghana a fact which is worthy of widespread understanding, namely, that not all white men are "bad" and all black men "good"—that black Africans can duplicate actions dubbed "tyrannical" and "oppressive" when performed by white men elsewhere in Africa.

But if independence has not yet turned Ghana into an African utopia with the perfect government which some of its critics seem to demand, neither the intellectuals like Henry nor the simple peasant tribesmen believe it is fair to label it a dictatorship. Certainly the libelous ferocity of some of its newspapers, the presence of a parliamentary opposition, and the vehemence of some opposition speakers appear to indicate considerable freedom of speech.

Perhaps Henry sums it up best: "Many of my people now are getting a more realistic idea of free-DOM. In other words, Ghanaians are beginning to see that independence merely means the right to make our own mistakes."

Nevertheless, some Africans elsewhere look longingly toward the kind of future Ghana represents. To Simon Mbatha, of Johannesburg, for example, it sometimes seems as though the African awakening has passed him by.

He is one of the 11 million nonwhites who live in the Union of South Africa. Elsewhere, Africans are being thrust to the fore in the dynamic upheaval which has overtaken much of this continent. There is talk of liberty, and human rights, and the freedom of the individual. But in South Africa it seems that Simon and his fellow Africans have yet to win a say in their own destiny.

For example, at one o'clock one morning, the people of Simon's township near Johnnesburg were sleeping peacefully.

Suddenly—bang, bang, bang on the doors of their frail tin shanties—and the police burst in. "Open up, open up. Where's your pass? Where's your working permit? Let's see your tax receipt. Where's your authorization to live in Johannesburg?" cries a young white policeman brandishing a revolver. Then: "Don't answer me back, you cheeky Kaffir, or you'll go to jail." Not much talk of human rights or the freedom of the individual here.

Simon's next-door neighbors, heavy with sleep, do go to jail, bundled in the police truck as their children wail in the empty house behind them.

Now it is 5 A.M. Simon is in the bus queue which winds away endlessly into the gray gloom of the dawn. The line edges forward around the great puddles and pools which the heavy rain is forming in the dirt road. Simon will wait more than an hour yet for his bus to work, for the transport service for Africans is inadequate, and few Africans own automobiles.

But Simon dares not risk being late for work and losing his job. It is a good job with good wages—nearly £5 ($14) a week—and it would be hard to find another like it.

Simon works in a garage and is a "stripper," which means that he is allowed to take certain pieces of cars apart, but may not fit them together again. That is work reserved for the white mechanics, and, although there is a shortage of skilled white mechanics and Simon's boss has told him that he, Simon, is a better mechanic than some of the new white men being taken on, his boss nevertheless dares not break the regulations and let Simon perform skilled work which he is able to do and with which he could treble or quadruple his present earnings.

Simon's employer is one of many white South Africans who feel deep sympathy for the African and who are concerned that he is denied the opportunity for advancing and uplifting himself by his own efforts.

There are many instances of white assistance to nonwhites and of different types of charitable work.

But there are, too, many white South Africans who have no concept of nonwhite existence, no personal knowledge of nonwhite hardships, and who honestly believe that reports of the misery suffered by many nonwhites are grossly exaggerated.

The fact is that it is exceedingly difficult for any white man to understand fully an African's thought processes until he, too, has experienced the unhappiness of racial discrimination—of shanty homes without electricity, sewerage, and water; of subeconomic wages which reduce children to poverty and hunger; of no franchise; of constant control by the police while enmeshed in a web of restrictive legislation which few Africans understand; and of an official segregation policy which provides facilities for nonwhites which are almost always inferior to those for whites, and sometimes nonexistent altogether.

This is a many-sided picture, of course, but this is Simon's

view of it, and these are the issues with which he and his
fellow Africans are mainly concerned in South Africa today.

Yet, while their prospects of political emancipation remain
dim, there is about these Africans a good humor and patience
and faith in the future which buoy them in time of trouble.
Whatever their immediate problems, their thoughts appear
unfettered.

Indeed, it sometimes seems as though there are more tension and fear for the future among Johannesburg's white men
on occasion than there are among the Africans who push on
despite their various problems.

7.

The story of peoples crawling, grinding, plunging ahead
does not end with Asia and Africa. In places where the advance began sooner, new stages are being reached. In Europe,
Australia, and the Americas, the poor are rising more and
more into the middle class. In some areas the middle class
knows living standards once reserved for the rich.

But, as world population leaps forward with hardly imaginable speed, both the richest and the poorest face the
consequences of certain simple facts. Of these, perhaps the
simplest—and most complex—is food. Abdul knows about it,
though, and from another point of view so does Everett
Larkin out in Kansas.

In 1958, Mr. Larkin had a good year. He pointed with pride
at the waving fields of grain marching off to the flat horizon:
"It's a good year. I'm going to build that addition to the
house, buy that second tractor, and get me one of those shiny
new cars." His optimistic views echoed the sentiments of
thousands of other wheat farmers in America's vital bread-
basket. United States officials placed the winter wheat crop
at a near record one billion bushels plus.

At the same time on the other side of the globe in the wide reaching plains of the Punjab of West Pakistan, Abdul (farmers seldom use last names) cultivated his wheat with a hand implement like that in use since before Alexander the Great invaded that part of the world. The farmer toiled on land he does not own. He, his wife, and five children share their mud and straw hut with an ox and two chickens. All members of the family evidence the effects of malnutrition, which limits their efficiency and production. They are deeply in debt. Partly because of the problems Abdul faces, Pakistan must import wheat (325,000 tons in 1956).

This, in nugget form, dramatizes the world's food picture today—overproduction and prosperity in some areas, underproduction and undernourishment in others.

And herein lies one of the major challenges to the world for the next half century—how better to distribute its food resources and to find a balance between population and food supply.

At the moment the problem looks staggering. Some 47 million new places have to be set yearly at the world's dining tables, which already accommodate some 2.8 billion persons. Total population may double in the next forty years.

International food experts estimate that at least one-half and perhaps as many as two-thirds of mankind live a "lifetime of malnutrition and actual hunger."

The Food and Agriculture Organization of the UN has pointed out an unsettling recent trend. Some of the best fed nations are becoming better fed, some of the worst fed, worse fed.

So far the graphs of rising food production and population have been nip and tuck. But there is a very serious threat that world harvest will fall behind the multiplying hungry mouths in the future. Once again debate rises over Malthus' famous and controversial theory (1798) that population always tends to outrun means of subsistence.

Earlier civilizations in Mesopotamia, Syria, Northwest China, and Central America disappeared in part, at least, because of failure of food sources.

In spite of the prodigious bounty of the United States cornucopia, it cannot feed the entire world. Problems of economics and distribution hamper such a solution.

And perhaps most importantly people must work out their own salvation insofar as they can. This is not just a philosophical viewpoint but also the statement of hardheaded food scientists who warn that the United States must be certain other countries do not become dependents.

Nevertheless, United States surpluses can and do help have-not nations out of food emergencies. For the year from May, 1957, to June, 1958, for example, shipments of surpluses totaled 5,828,000 metric tons.

In the opinion of many food experts, the United States surplus is only a temporary phenomenon. That is, within ten or twenty years, they estimate, its own crop of babies will overtake the harvest in its fields.

Furthermore, around the world food-yielding lands are deteriorating and eroding. Even the United States is reaching limits of its arable lands, and great areas of its soils are leaching out.

Yet food scientists are confident that supplies can be increased by higher productivity on present land, reclamation of new land, and improved agricultural practices.

In fact the dinner table of the future may be set with a variety of foods unknown today. Algae, plankton, food yeasts, sugars from wood wastes, a wide range of sea foods by industrial "farming," and perhaps many mass-produced foods from factories using photosynthesis (combining air, sunlight, water, and mineral as plants do) may well be on the bill of fare.

Also in the future the world may organize agriculture in such a fashion that products will be grown in places where they grow best, disregarding national boundaries.

Insecticides, good seed, fertilizers, better planting practices, and modern agricultural implements offer hope for increasing production in the near future.

Modern technology does not mean necessarily highly complicated and expensive equipment. To an Asian peasant cultivating his plot on his knees with a short-handled hoe, it may mean just a long-handled hoe. Scythes are more efficient than sickles in many farm operations. These items have the advantage that they can be fashioned in village shops.

In the world as a whole, six out of ten persons live on farms and depend on agriculture for a livelihood. It varies from continent to continent, with the United States figure two out of ten. In Latin America more than six, and in Asia and Africa seven or more, out of ten work on the land.

Yet only about 5 to 7 per cent of the world's surface is suitable for agriculture.

World staples are wheat, corn, rice, and meat. Rice is by far the most important single crop. About half the world population depends on it.

One of the major problems of underdeveloped nations is the vicious circle of deprivation. The people of these countries are too undernourished to work hard. Therefore they are able to grow only a mere subsistence which, in turn, keeps them undernourished.

Areas of plenty include North America, Argentina, the United Kingdom, Ireland, Scandinavia, and the Benelux countries. Most of Europe has fair food supplies. But all Asia and parts of Africa have very inadequate supplies. Large sections of Latin America are little better off.

The main difficulty in the Orient is too little food production per person. Some areas produce well. But too many must be fed from one acre. China has less than one-third acre of cultivated land per person, India about one acre.

In parts of Latin America Indians chew coca leaves, which dulls their senses and enables them to work long hours without food.

FAO officials are considering a plan for a year's intensive campaign against hunger on a global scale. Under the plan, specialized agencies of the UN and national and international organizations would be mobilized to fight want. It would be an effort similar to the International Geophysical Year.

FAO experts concede that a year is a short time to do much about solving world food problems. But they say that such a drive could heighten awareness of the problems of hunger and poverty and improve the means of action to meet those problems.

Improvement of food production in underdeveloped countries is a major objective of technical assistance programs of the United States, the UN, and private organizations.

One of the most dramatic demonstrations of technical assistance took place in Mexico during the 1940's when the Rockefeller Foundation introduced improved corn seed and new hybrids suited to the Mexican soil and climate. Within a few years Mexico became a corn-exporting country. It formerly imported this staple.

But this comparatively swift progress is unusual. There is no element of world population more conservative and tradition-bound than the farmer, tied by the weight of centuries to his ancestors' methods.

And yet Point Four workers and international technicians have been able slowly to change ancient patterns of thought and bring about increased production.

In India, for example, technicians have found that if they can convince a family respected in a small village to grow rice in a new and more efficient method, the new technique will take hold quite fast.

However, it frequently takes longer to seed men's minds with new ideas and techniques than it does to change outmoded methods.

Although technical assistance programs have had spectacular failures as well as successes, there is a backbone of selfless specialists working to improve the lot of peasants in Central America or Thailand, Bolivia or Iran, and doing a major missionary work for better production that is invaluable.

What is certain is that inefficient food production methods in many countries must change if teeming populations are to be fed in the future.

Political decisions have major impact on food production. Since World War II several units (such as Pakistan) have spun off into independence with areas too small to maintain themselves economically. This flies in the face of the fact that modern agricultural technology requires large areas.

In Argentina, under dictator Juan Domingo Perón, agriculture was de-emphasized. Industry, some of it completely uneconomic, was fostered. This proud rich pampaland, which used to build up tremendous wealth through its sales of cattle and grains abroad, found itself virtually destitute after a decade of such ill-conceived planning.

The United States is presently in a stage of explosive food

production even though it is heading into a period of less acreage with industries, highways, airports, and suburbs swallowing more and more farm land. Yet new technologies make poor land fertile, supplemental irrigation lessens dependence on rainfall, and merging of smaller units into bigger farms produces higher quality management. The end result: towering surpluses.

Surpluses for the present, at least, are a great potential, many believe. They are the one resource which the Soviets do not have yet. However, one need is for more efficient use of local currencies earned by surplus sales abroad.

Surpluses, however, must be used wisely to help underdeveloped nations feed themselves where this is possible, food experts warn. The United States cannot provide food for ever-burgeoning populations around the world.

If, for example, foodstuffs are shipped abroad and sold for local currencies which are used for a carefully worked out irrigation project, food can be used thereby to increase productivity of land. This money also might be used to buy more fertilizers or farm tools.

Surpluses create major international difficulties for the United States. Other main agricultural countries, such as Canada, Australia, New Zealand, the Netherlands, and Argentina, bitterly protest United States subsidized "dumping" of goods which they also sell in the world market.

There is no indispensable food, according to scientists at the Massachusetts Institute of Technology. According to these scientists, human beings require some four dozen nutrients including vitamins, minerals, amino acids, and calories. It doesn't matter where these nutrients come from.

Milk, for example, is an excellent source of calcium. But the Mexican and Central American staple, the tortilla, dating back to pre-Colombian times, is equally rich in that mineral.

Nor is it necessary to eat animal foods in order to be well nourished, according to these scientists, althought they qualify this statement by adding that it is easier to get the required nutrients from meat.

The fact is there is not enough land in the world to produce a North American diet for the rest of the world.

At times too much emphasis is placed on solving food-growing problems by creating big irrigation projects, some specialists believe. The question they face is what use to make of the land served by the dam. Many times the answer, they find, does not make a positive contribution to the nation's food supply.

West Pakistan offered land near one of its new irrigation projects to the highest bidders, who turned out to be the rich who then planted the land to sugar. While it gave employment, it did not provide land for the landless or add greatly to the essential foods of the nation.

In Iran, Shah Mohammed Riza Pahlevi worked out plans to distribute land he held. A tract of land was carved into equal parts without regard to its varying quality and productivity. The landless then were turned onto it without buildings, equipment, stock, or materials. An agricultural bank was set up to lend money but did not have sufficient resources. Since that experiment, land problems in Iran have been handled more efficiently.

Similar land resettlement programs elsewhere in the world have failed for lack of careful planning.

The over-all problem of world food supplies is not just the subject of empty debate. It is a vital issue that affects everyone and certainly will absorb more planning and thought in the future as new multitudes throng this spinning globe.

8.

Abdul will be there among the multitudes, among the earth's awakening peoples. Where do we of the privileged nations fit into his future? Perhaps a California housewife can give us a clue.

When Mrs. William Gres, of Los Angeles, looks squarely at her country's international responsibility to freedom, she says spontaneously, "It's just like raising a family!"

Mrs. Gres is an aircraft worker's wife and a very happy, gracious lady. Her husband got into aircraft manufacture as soon as he finished high school and now he is superintendent of manufacturing for North American Aviation's big Los Angeles plant. The Greses have two lovely daughters.

One might expect to find Mrs. Gres saying that world leadership costs too much. The Gres family live in a fine house—with high taxes. They have a brand new swimming pool that the tax assessor has already scrutinized calculatingly.

But Mrs. Gres said earnestly, "I never did object to taxes. When you consider all we have in America, you simply can't say our taxes are high."

Asked whether in her opinion the United States is doing enough to help other countries develop economically, she answered, "Yes, I think we are doing as much as we should." But after considering a moment she added, "Maybe we should be doing even more.

"Maybe we should be giving other countries more direct help—not just money.

"It's like raising a family," Mrs. Gres continued. "There are some things you just can never pay other people to do for your children. You must do it yourself. We ought to help other people more through direct contact."

Mrs. Gres's world outlook has grown with her own experience. During World War II, North American sent her husband to its plant in Dallas. She loved Dallas, every minute of it—she'd never been away from California before—but she hadn't been there twenty-four hours before she had been called "Yankee" twice.

It made her realize, Mrs. Gres indicated, what it may mean to feel strange or foreign to other people.

"Bill and I have some very close friends who were escapees from Hungary," she said. "They are thrilled with the United States, but every now and then they seem a bit rebellious over all the things Americans have when there are so many needy people in the world."

It shows, she commented, how great a work Americans can do to emphasize real values—the things people learn to appreciate in each other from direct contact.

Mrs. Gres has done her stint of Girl Scout and PTA work, and loved it. Now that the girls are in junior and senior high schools, she has enough free time so she can spend a day each week as a volunteer worker at Good Samaritan Hospital. It's an Episcopal institution—the Greses are Presbyterians. This summer the girls will serve there, too, as "Candy Stripers," helping nurses in the wards.

"I get lots of satisfaction out of this," Mrs. Gres said. "You learn so much from helping people."

"But when it gets done on a world scale," a visitor asked, "isn't there lots of waste?"

"Oh, there is so much waste in both public and private enterprise!" Mrs. Gres exclaimed. "You know how it is in the aircraft business—sometimes tremendous amounts of money go for nothing. But in so many things there is no other way of learning. I think the old saying is true: 'Experience is the best teacher.'

"It's the future we must think about. We spend big amounts of money for schools and for government—it's all investment in the future."

Mrs. Gres is delighted that her girls are beginning to have the kind of school experience involving young people from various racial and cultural backgrounds. This is a new experience for their neighborhood because boys and girls are brought in by bus from other school districts. Some people are anxious about it.

"But I tell the girls we just cannot go through life avoiding experiences with people who are different," their mother said.

How do Mrs. Gres and her husband keep informed about world affairs? Bill Gres works long hours and many nights has to go back to the plant after dinner. They don't find time, she said, for nearly as much reading as they would like; they have almost no time, she said regretfully, for books.

They subscribe to magazines—*Newsweek, Life*, the *Atlantic Monthly, Reader's Digest*. When they can, they look at television, especially the Sunday interview and debate shows. They especially enjoy "Wide Wide World" and Ed Murrow.

"I think I'm an optimist," Mrs. Gres concluded.

What she meant, she made plain, is that she sees the same thing working to form her own outlook that she sees needful in the world—increased caring by individuals for individuals, as in a family. And as in a family, the caring grows as the responsibilities increase, but nobody thinks to fear it, so Mrs. Gres could see no reason why Americans should fear their widening world responsibilities.

As with Americans, so with anyone who is better off than his neighbors in a shrinking world. The solution to the problems of the future begins with something as simple as a family feeling for mankind.

MAN AND NATURE

More Triumphs Ahead

1.

THOUGH HUMANITY STILL BINDS ITSELF WITH IGNORANCE, PAS-sion, and fear, it has progressively widened its freedom from material limitations. All the indications are that, unless men fail to control themselves, they will spectacularly further their domination of nature in the future.

From better dishwashing to better atomic fission, the advance of technology is already in full surge. In one country the future may mean automation; in another, simply the more efficient use of the bullock. We can see tomorrow in what is happening today.

Take the mass media, which in one way or another affect us all. Take that nonexistent "typical American" George Arbuthnot in Middletown, U.S.A.

It is about 6:30 A.M. and George is drifting through the final moments that link his sleeping to his waking hours.

Already the sun is dappling the wallpaper above his head. But it is not the sun that wakes him up, nor the barking of a dog down the street.

On the bedside table beside him the hands of a clock-radio reach exactly six thirty. Music begins to pour faintly, then more loudly from the speaker.

George awakes, not to the sights and sounds of the actual world but to the voices of the synthetic world of mass communications—the world within a world in which men today spend so large and significant a part of their lives, connected to events and other people by barely dry newsprint and the jungles of electronic tubes that they (and their repairmen) have come to take for granted.

On this particular morning, it suddenly occurs to George that his waking sets the pattern for his day—a pattern dependent at nearly every turn upon mass media for information and guidance.

For example, to find out what to wear, he leaves his radio on while he shaves and learns how warm the day will be and whether it will rain. Before he can snap it off, the radio also advises him what brand of raincoat he should have bought, and what toothpaste to brush with before he goes down to breakfast.

At the breakfast table the world of toast and marmalade competes with that of the morning newspaper, a world built up from football scores, columns of Washington pundits, wire photos from Paris, cablegrams from the Middle East, projecting him—as George points out excitedly to his neglected wife—far beyond the few feet of space his body occupies and his physical senses report upon.

George continues to dwell on his new discovery while he drives to work, half-soothed, half-distracted by the disk-jockey chatter and sales talk from his car radio.

As he approaches his office from the parking lot, he notices that he is becoming the target for the purposeful sights and sounds of city streets, the guerrilla outposts of the mass communicators.

Garish magazine covers bombard his attention at corner newsstands. Movie posters leap out at him with scenes he will not see on the screen if he goes inside. Sound trucks assault his ears with news of giant sales.

When he looks up, he sees a skywriting plane advertising automobiles. When he looks down, he finds VOTE FOR MC-EVOY FOR CITY COUNCIL stenciled on the sidewalk at his feet.

In just a few hundred yards, dozens of messages, printed, pictorial, and vocal, are addressed to him as a citizen, as a consumer of goods and services, and as a human being presumed to be in present need of entertainment.

George absorbs these messages almost automatically, as he did the day before, as he will do tomorrow. But he wonders: What effect do they have on his political opinions, on his standards of taste, on his notions of what makes the good life? The question troubles him, and at lunchtime he begins to think of his wife, Alice.

Though Alice does not leave the house all day, she is receiving, he knows, even more "messages" than he. This is the day, he recalls, that two women's magazines come through the mail slot, invading the home (which he bought because these magazines approved) with new ideas about how he should furnish it, the clothes he should wear, and what he should eat.

Along with thousands of other husbands across the land, he will have a dessert recipe tried on him tonight because a food editor has assured her 5 million readers that "men will love it."

George sighs at the thought. But he understands that Alice gets more than recipes and decorating formulas from her magazines, her radio soap operas, and her "three-handkerchief" movies. They give her, as she often says, companionship. Through them she shares, however superficially and melodramatically, the experiences common to women and not just housekeepers.

While driving home from work, George also has time to think about his son George, Jr. The youngsters, he reflects, bear the brunt of the age of technology in mass communications—as elsewhere.

Like most adolescents, George, Jr., is hungry for a code to accept and follow. In the mass media, George realizes, he finds his models.

Junior spent an inordinate amount of time this morning combing his hair like his favorite Western hero. He has adopted the walk of the football player who scored three touchdowns on television last Saturday, and he is beginning to dismay his parents with a laugh, which—they have just learned—is the trademark of an animated cartoon rabbit.

But mass communications also play a less trivial role in his life. He has a friend with an FM radio and an LP collection, and he is at least being exposed to classical music.

Furthermore, an appetite for science-fiction, first fed by comic and pulp magazines, has led him to a real interest in physics and math.

Next spring an educational TV channel will be started in a near-by city, and at least one of his courses in school will be taught through television over a closed circuit.

George recognizes that his son is better informed on a wider variety of subjects than he was at fifteen, thanks to the mass media. But he is still a bit afraid of them. They are so insistent and so pervasive.

In the evening he visits his public library. He learns from the statistical reference shelf that there are more than 40 million American homes with television, in which sets are watched an estimated 2.6 billion man-hours a week (as compared with 1.9 billion man-hours spent in gainful employment).

That there are 128 million radios in the country, tuned in more than two hours daily.

That 46 million Americans still attend the movies in the course of a week, leaving an annual gross of more than a billion dollars at the boxoffices.

That United States newspapers have a circulation of over 130 million; magazines, about 450 million.

He walks home in the crisp autumn evening, glad to smell the leaves and count the stars—grateful for a little solitude and quiet. He sees how the mass media can distract him from this kind of experience, giving him living only at second hand. He remembers from college days Plato's image of the cave and he wonders if he is too often looking at the shadows of people and events.

He sees that every day he is in danger of receiving too many facts, impressions, and messages, so that his responses may be dulled and everything reduced to the same level. He understands, too, that the major media of communications are truly mass-distributing, so that people about him are receiving virtually the same messages as he; and he instinctively dreads the standardization that tends to result.

But as he sets his clock-radio for tomorrow, he realizes there is no turning back. He could not do without his newspaper, his radio, or his television set even if he wanted to. Like atomic energy, they are a given factor in his experience —a power that he has the freedom to apply wisely or not.

He can use mass communications selectively to stimulate his interest in the world about him. Or he can glut himself on entertainment until the world he is most familiar with is a sealed-off hothouse of electronic dream-images.

It is not a choice that can be easily dramatized. It will be a matter which he and his family must settle quietly and

inwardly, day by day. But few other choices, he realizes, will
be more important to his own moral and intellectual health
—and therefore, that of his country.

2.

The mass media, of course, have invaded not only America
but the whole world. And the responsibility for the best use
of them does not rest solely on the George Arbuthnots, the
"consumers" of mass communications, but also on the pro-
ducers.

Within five minutes after the Supreme Court of the United
States had delivered its famous school desegregation decision in 1954, that momentous information was on its way to
the remotest corners of the globe. Within an hour it was on
the radios of Asia, Africa, and Oceania. And a few minutes
thereafter it was a topic of warm discussion in a thousand
mudhut villages, where previously not one villager in five
hundred had heard of the Supreme Court.

In this and in countless other ways there is shown the
amazing change which has come over the world in the matter
of communication between and among men. Today mankind's thoughts and reactions are being molded not only with
a speed but with a depth and breadth which would have
been deemed impossible a few decades ago.

Thus it is not only legitimate but actually vitally important
for all of us to consider whether the communications media
are living up to their highest potential, whether they are adequately serving the great goals of brotherhood, peace, well-
being, morality, and mutual understanding.

We owe it to ourselves to ask to what extent radio, television, newspapers, magazines, and book publishers are providing humanity with those facts which are needed for sound
personal, local, national, and international decisions, to what

extent they are stressing the hopeful and helpful aspects of
mankind's endeavors, and to what extent they are aiding
rather than hindering the world's efforts to rise above those
conditions which would keep it warlike, poor, ignorant, and
and unhappy.

It is no secret that each of these media has its bitter de-
tractors and its strong defenders. Furthermore, each point of
view can marshal powerful arguments to support its points.
One can analyze press, radio, and television, for example, and
come away convinced that their influence is nefarious, that
they cater in the main to the lowest interests of mankind, that
they are woefully failing to use their immense potential for
good.

On the other hand, and taking a historic point of view,
one could argue that never before have people been given
so much or so exact information, that there has been a steady
long-term upward trend in news, entertainment, and information, and that mass communication media are today
doing just about what might be expected of them, given the
world in which they operate.

Both of these viewpoints are, it would seem, correct. It is
undeniable that all means of communication could do considerably more than at present to support the higher efforts of
humanity. They could devote more time to cultural subjects.
They could deal less with sensationalism and more with the
constructive aspects of local, national, and international news.
They could be more courageous and farsighted in their
efforts to lead the public rather than be led by it. They could
more surely make themselves spokesmen for the worthy
causes which abound. They could emphasize the wholesome
in entertainment and eschew the degrading.

Yet, it is undeniable that there is much to applaud both in
the present attitude of these communications media and in

their progress toward greater civic and moral responsibility. Consider for a moment the press. Despite the fact that many newspapers still sensationalize the worthless and harmful, despite the widespread display of crime, sex, and disaster, there are few papers today which display the irresponsibility of the age of yellow journalism. Newspapers may be tamer, but they are also more conscientious, fair and, in many ways, courageous.

Whatever criticism there may be of the press, it is overshadowed by the much more articulate criticism directed toward radio and television, particularly the latter.

One newspaper reviewer of television programs estimates that not more than 15 per cent of time and probably nearer 10 per cent is devoted not to what is sometimes called "longhair stuff," but to ordinary programs of an instructive nature, such as good drama, the better music, and informative news. The rest of the time is devoted to programs of an "escapist" nature.

Many television executives are aware of this and regret the fact. They claim, however, that their attempts to lead in an opposite direction have failed in enough instances to make them wary. Yet they speak with legitimate pride of the amount of time which they devoted to the Kefauver crime hearings, the McCarthy hearings, and several United Nations debates on major issues. They also state that they have refused to cut into many of their news programs, even though faced with more lucrative offers for the time.

Yet the weight of evidence seems to be on the side of those who say that television, unlike the press, has not measured up to its obligations as adequately as the public has a right to demand. A notable exception to this judgment is, of course, those stations which are of an educational nature and which largely devote themselves to cultural and educational features. Unfortunately, the audience for such stations seems to be small.

This, in turn, leads to the question as to how far each of the various communications media has had the courage to lead public opinion and taste. It is generally felt that newspapers and the book publishing industry have been more courageous in this matter than have television, radio or motion pictures.

Is this due to the fact that journalism and literature are so much older and therefore so much more mature than are the other three?

There are those who assert that it is unreasonable to demand of mass communications media that they be leaders in public service. These indivduals say that such media, like other major aspects of public life, seek the level of the general public and reflect its tastes and abilities. They claim still further that public standards have not progressed as swiftly as has technological discovery and that, as a consequence, the human aspect of communication has not kept pace with the scientific. But, they add, the pressures generated by scientific discovery are forcing public interest and standards to advance more rapidly than in the past and, with the passing of years, we shall find the level of television and radio rising as we have with newspapers.

It is clearly the obligation of those who maintain and direct these media to facilitate whenever and wherever possible this advance in standards and service and not to hold back either through timidity or avarice.

These are some of the large challenges that advanced communications will carry along into the future. What are some of the specific new electronic devices we can expect? As the telephone replaces the signal drum in Africa, what is coming to peoples further along the road of technological progress?

In the first place, communications are going to become more personal for all of us. At the same time, communications—pictures, sound and printed matter—are going to be more widespread.

There seems little doubt that our homes, if we wish, can have "communications centers" of their own. The nucleus of these new "communications" is there now in our telephone, television, and radio receivers and high-fidelity and tape machines. These instruments, enlarged in some of their functions and combined, are going to produce the "central" home communications system of the future.

Not only are these communications bound to bring the world into our living rooms but they seem destined to keep track of the whereabouts of members of the family unit.

To give some specific examples:

The home television set is now a very one-sided affair bringing in "information" from one direction. As a "closed circuit" device in the home, the same receiver—through technical advances now feasible—may be used by a mother to check on a sleeping child in an upstairs room, on chidren playing out of doors, or to determine who the caller is at the door.

Employing the closed-circuit principle through the so-called "community antenna systems," the home TV receiver could "dial" the local movie house to "see" the picture showing there, or "visit" the local library for reference material. Or the householder could visit the local "film library" where he would receive tape relays of television shows and motion pictures.

Under new high-fidelity tape recording techniques, the electronic signals from TV cameras or motion-picture cameras using iconoscopes as their "eyes" rather than lenses and films could be reproduced directly from a tape reel connected to the home TV set or through a community cable system linking the film library with the home television receiver.

In between the frustratingly short bulletinized news reports of the radio and television stations and the full accounts carried by the newspapers lies a field for much expanded reports of news and pictures of world events, to be made available in the home.

The home FM (frequency modulation) receiver is the key to the home newspaper. Equipped with rolls of photosensitive paper and a recording stylus actuated by signals over the FM band, the home FM set would be able to deliver in the home a substantial "newspaper."

The home newspaper set would go into action at 1 A.M. when the family was in bed. Between then and 6 A.M. it would be able to produce an appreciable amount of news and pictures. A householder on a particularly stormy morning when the paperboy had been unable to get around would merely come down to his "facsimile printer" and update himself.

The telephone, that ubiquitous instrument which we live by and with, is rapidly becoming a more personalized communication channel. Transistors now make possible a telephone receiver, combined with a transmitter if wanted, about the size of a cake of laundry soap, powered with batteries.

With this personal telephone receiver-transmitter one may conduct a two-way conversation. With the two-way portable telephone the salesman and his office manager, the reporter and his editor will be able to reach each other either directly by radio channels, or through regular telephone communication channels, as do the patrolman and his sergeant, taxi drivers and utility men and their offices.

Another type of telephonic device is the one-way "paging" set. With this type of set, the receivers carried by each of the above individuals may be selectively rung. The paged person would then go to a telephone and call to find out what the message was.

The biggest problem in employing this personal communication depends on the so-far scant availability of suitable radio frequencies.

Today, it is technically possible to have picture transmission so that telephone users can see the persons with whom they are talking. Pictures, however, require a much wider band of frequencies. Until the telephone laboratories devise a more economical method of sending picture signals, telephone TV will be sharply limited.

At present telephone TV is too expensive for anything but conferences or meetings and limited personal uses. However, the transistor again has come to the aid of picture telephone. Since it uses less power than a vacuum tube, the transistor-amplifier carrying a wider range of frequencies, can be powered over the wires used to carry the voice and picture signals.

The urgent need for economy in the radio spectrum, especially in the transmission of pictures, indicates that these signals may have to be condensed or reduced to the same type of electronic information that computers employ.

Through these means, and with the aid of "information theory"—which means telling us the least amount of "information" that can be sent and still preserve intelligibility—great amounts of condensed signals can be sent. The apparatus at the other end, whether it be a TV set, a radio receiver or a facsimile printer, will be able to take these reduced signals and reproduce the missing portions.

The transistor may even lead to wafer-thin portable TV receivers, possibly operated with batteries.

These portable television sets, which will resemble thin glass building blocks, can also be operated off extension cords plugged into regular house electrical systems, or be plugged into the car dashboard. Already cars have radio sets, shavers, extension lights, and percolators operating off their batteries.

Earth satellites plus the larger space vehicles that are expected to be launched will give man a "leg up" on worldwide communication. By the use of so-called "scatter" propagation techniques, world-wide television is now possible. "Scatter" transmissions send signals up at the electrified "blankets" or layers above the earth's surface. Some of this energy bounces back, like a ray of light hitting a mirror, to be picked up at extremely long distances.

3.

In the United States the advances in communications will no doubt be accompanied by improved electric dishwashers, gas clothes dryers, radar rotisseries, and undreamed of laborsaving devices providing more time to use still more laborsaving devices. But if "capitalist" Americans sometimes seem to be dwindling into slaves of their gadgets, the citizens of Communist Russia also face a future complicated by machines. Here is the way one Moscow family went to meet that future:

Moving day finally dawned chill and gray. Nadyezhda Pavlovna Leskova, excused from her teaching job for the occasion, glanced uneasily at the sluggish overcast, freighted with snow, or, worse still perhaps, the first April showers. The truck was coming at ten o'clock and she pictured her worldly effects reduced to sogginess in the hour's drive across Mos-

cow from Marina Roscha to the Lenin Hills. But rain or shine
there could be no postponement. Meanwhile, there was
plenty to worry about besides the weather.

For weeks, in anticipation of this crucial day, Nadyezhda
Pavlovna mentally had been sorting out the things to be left
behind when they vacated the two rooms in the old wooden
house where she and her family had lived almost twenty
years. Like most housewives, she hated to part with objects
that were like old and faithful friends. But her husband,
Nikolai Maximovich Leskov, a construction engineer at the
State Planning Commission, had been categorical.

"We are not just moving into a new abode," he intoned in
the rhetorical style he brought home from the office along
with his briefcase. "We are moving into a new era, a new
stage in our progress toward a brighter future. And I don't
want this future cluttered up with a lot of useless, outmoded
junk. I don't care whether you sell it, give it away, throw it
away, or burn it."

As usual, Nadyezhda Pavlovna concurred and began making lists. She had been over the floor plan of the new three-
room flat carefully, and had visited the construction site several times. With running water and a bathroom, they would-
n't require the old portable tin bathtub, or the wooden washstand with its cracked mirror and porcelain basin with the
flower design. These objects had stood in their corner behind
a screen so long that frequent wetting had rotted the floor-
boards. Then there was the massive, cast-iron *burzhuika*
stove, with its lengths of pipe, coal scuttle, and assorted tongs
and implements. None of these would be needed in the new
flat.

For besides plumbing, it had central heating and gas. So it
was good-by forever to the cumbersome equipment and

heavy work involved in hauling water and keeping warm. Also slated for the discard were the two sooty *kerosinkas* on which Nadyezhda Pavlovna and her mother had cooked the meals in the cluttered communal kitchen. The two women, almost out of a sense of loyalty, had suggested taking the kerosene stoves along for eventual use in the country *dacha*. But Nikolai Maximovich, when he learned of this, had objected and promised them instead a new double-burner primus by summer.

The real problem was with borderline items, the utility of which could be argued, like the massive oak wardrobe that had been in Nadyezhda Pavlovna's family for generations. She had wept and pleaded unavailingly. Nikolai Maximovich reminded her that the new flat had built-in closets—so why sacrifice living space to that bulky heirloom?

"We don't intend to establish a museum," he concluded.

The weeding-out process was especially painful to Nadyezhda Pavlovna's mother, as though she herself were being consigned to the discard, a victim of technological unemployment. For she was the family's *babushka* (grandmother) and as such held a most pivotal position in the household at Marina Roscha. As with many Soviet families where both husband and wife have jobs and which lack either the space or the means to keep a maid, the Leskovs through the years had depended on Babushka to do the marketing, cook most of the meals, mend the clothes, do the chores, and baby sit.

Since the children were grown, Babushka's workload had lightened considerably and she spent all her evenings from six thirty to eleven o'clock glued to her chair in front of the TV set. Whatever the program, she lost herself in it completely and talked back to the announcers and actors with pithy comments that delighted her grandchildren.

The TV set was the family's first important bridgehead in modern living many months before they moved from Marina Roscha. There had been no room for a refrigerator, but Nikolai Maximovich had ordered one for the new flat. This meant that in warm weather the family would no longer have to buy food on a hand-to-mouth basis.

But Babushka, who stood to benefit the most, was not altogether happy at the prospect. She loved to break the monotony by shuffling off to market and the stores several times a day on various errands and pretexts, gossiping and chatting with the peasants, salesclerks, and other *babushkas* out shopping like herself. She was almost terrified by the thought of a separate kitchen all to herself. She would be terribly lonely with no neighbors to talk to, as in the communal kitchen.

"What if something goes wrong," she complained, "say gas starts escaping, and I'm in there alone, how can I get help?"

Babushka also had misgivings about the bathtub and its gas-operated hot water geyser. She vowed she would continue her weekly visits to the public bath as heretofore, even though it involved a long trek from the Lenin Hills back to Marina Roscha. Babushka was like the old Romans in this respect. She went to the public bath not just to bathe, but to meet and gossip with her friends, other *babushkas*, while they steamed and scrubbed themselves, and she viewed the bath in the new flat as another encroachment on her habits.

Nikolai Maximovich, bent on launching the new way of life with a flourish, had splurged on new furniture and assorted electric appliances, including a small clothes washer, a vacuum cleaner, and an East German electric coffee pot. Nadyezhda Pavlovna had chided him for such extravagance.

"People will start talking about you behind your back, wondering where you got the money."

"Supposing a few envious tongues do wag," he retorted. "The time is past when people were put away merely because somebody denounced them."

"I hope you're right," was all Nadyezhda Pavlovna would answer.

At first Babushka would have no truck with the new electrical gadgets, despite the promptings of Nikolai Maximovich, who, when he came home from work, trotted them out and proceeded to explain and demonstrate. In his patient effort to break down her resistance, he marshaled quotations from *Pravda*. Had not Nikita S. Khrushchev proclaimed that the Soviet Union was to outstrip America? It was Babushka's patriotic duty to contribute to this national effort by mastery of the vacuum cleaner and washing machine. Failure to do this would be equivalent to sabotage.

Babushka had a strong respect for government policy and a sense of patriotism. The last thing she wanted to be accused of was sabotage. Consequently she gradually resigned herself to the appliances. She didn't entirely make her peace with them. It was more like an uneasy truce, with lingering suspicion that they were likely to explode or burst into flame or electrocute one. She always insisted on having Nadyezhda Pavlovna, Nikolai Maximovich, or one of the children connect the plugs. When she was alone in the house, she never went near the gadgets.

While Babushka and in some instances Nadyezhda Pavlovna dragged their feet, the Leskov youngsters, Tolya, aged fourteen and Galya, aged thirteen, accepted the new era with enthusiasm. Nikolai Maximovich soon discovered that in their case his missionary zeal on behalf of modern living had unleashed appetites he hadn't bargained for. One day Tolya came home from school and triumphantly announced that as part of his eighth-grade automotive course he had passed his driver's test. The instruction included driving a beat-up Moskvich around the school yard. While he couldn't get a license until he was eighteen, he could drive with an adult sitting next to him, if only he had a car.

After these preliminaries he popped the main question: "Why don't we get our own Moskvich?"

Before Nikolai Maximovich could answer, Galya chimed in. Why not? Her girl friend Vera's father had one, so did Anyusha's.

"Just imagine," she said, warming to the subject. "We could ride out to the country on Sundays, go picnicking, swimming, mushroom hunting. Or we could drive in town to the theater. It's so far and the Metro won't be finished for at least another two years."

Nadyezhda Pavlovna, for once, took a firm stand in favor of the children. Vainly Nikolai Maximovich pleaded economy. His wife pointedly replied that he would have done better to have bought a car in the first place rather than so much furniture. Oddly enough it was Babushka, the family's arch-conservative, who settled the argument. She announced that she had 18,000 rubles on her savings book which she had planned to divide between the children when they got married. But if nobody objected she was willing to use it to finance the purchase of a Moskvich, which cost 16,000 rubles.

His defense thus outflanked, Nikolai Maximovich, still grumbling about extravagance, surrendered. Since then the Leskovs have placed an order for a Moskvich. Their number will not come up for two years. But the youngsters are confident that under their constant prodding Nikolai Maximovich will find a short cut, and with this in view they are already planning a motor trip to the Caucasus next year.

4.

In comparison to the Leskovs, most Americans have had little trouble in acquiring gadgets. Their problem is to keep from being overcome by their possessions, as in the black predictions of their critics, both foreign and domestic.

But already there are signs that the American concern with gadgets—as distinct from the sensible use of gadgets—is close to, or may even have passed, its peak. To be sure, in the future Americans may have more gadgets than they now have, but they probably will think less about them.

People will depend on them less to win prestige, or to keep up with the Joneses—because the Joneses won't be depending so much on gadgets to help them keep up with the Smiths.

More and more, as with business success itself, the gadget is seen as giving a person extra time in which to win status, distinction, a sense of true individuality, through achievements in fields other than the production and use of gadgets.

Up to now much of the time saved by one set of gadgets has been expended on another set. And even when this set was mostly recreational—like television, or radio, or movies, or the family car—it has exercised the same influences for standardization of daily experience and responses.

More and more persons are becoming aware of this. There may be said to have developed in the last few years a "revolt of the individual" against the conformity which an obsessive regard for material objects has imposed on daily life.

One interesting sign of this was a recent report in a national magazine. It told of a social researcher who had decided to go into the public-relations business with a new approach. This was to be based on the idea that "status symbols" change in society: what gives a person a sense of prestige and standing in the community at one time may later be found inadequate for this purpose; businessmen need guidance to adjust themselves to these changes.

Back of this change at the moment is a sense that personal possessions, particularly items of "ostentatious consumption" —being available to "too many" persons—now have lost their power to confer distinction, which of course depends on one's not being like "the many."

Seen in the oversimplified way that public-relations men often must try to see things, this change appears to indicate only that people will be seeking distinction through better housing and more tasteful homes in future.

The "switch" is expected as a reaction against too-large and too-finny automobiles and other visible but superfluous appurtenances of a bank account or an installment-credit rating. But an assumption that this change means only a switch of interest from one sort of material products to another sort of material products would be a very superficial diagnosis indeed.

The Adam Smiths and the John Stuart Mills long ago pointed out that the economic release of mankind from dawn-till-dusk drudgery was a necessary prelude to their desiring nonmaterial advances. A man with an hour to think began to think of freedom, of dignity, and of human rights. Even before the shortening of the work day, the coming of adequate lighting for houses gave whole families additional hours in which to read and talk about what they read. Great social and political reforms followed.

Today, as in Adam Smith's century, we can see man impelled by his distinctive moral energies to provide the material means for their ever-wider exercise, for an ever-expanding field of consciousness. We see men and women never content merely to adapt themselves to a present physical environment as most living organisms have done through the ages, but insisting on changing that environment, and always aware that the environment needing change includes an endless conglomeration of personal and group relationships, beliefs, habits, vested interests, oppression, indifference—all nonmaterial factors.

East or West, the individual who comes under the influence of technological advances in travel, communications, labor on the farm, in the factory or home, is an individual whose physical burdens are lessening but whose mental tasks appear to be getting more and more complex and pressing.

But it is all too easy to attribute these problems simply to technological progress. They really rest in the individual's attitude. It is a mistake to think that people in highly mechanized civilizations are the only ones to come under stress from their social and economic ways of life. In primitive societies—even those characterized by a lack of understanding of the urgency of regular work—the sense of social and supernatural stress on the individual may be as destructively heavy as the stresses of machine society.

While important changes of attitude toward material symbols and instruments of well-being have been occurring in the United States, people in other lands have been catching up somewhat with Americans on the equipment front. But perhaps at less cost culturally than usually is associated with the American advance. In Europe especially there is a certain resistance, mostly among the more advantaged and educated classes, to "durable consumer goods."

It comes partly from a deeper commitment to traditional ways of life than ever existed in the United States. It is abetted by a much less well-developed system of consumer credit. Also, lower wage scales in industry have left at least a vestige of the old servant class still available for domestic duty.

The social, as distinct from functional, requirement to have a maid, or at least a "char," begins at a lower income level in Britain, for example, than in the United States.

And in older societies a sense of obligation on the part of the employing classes toward people who have mastered no other occupation than domestic service often prompts the employment of these people instead of the purchase of a laborsaving device.

Yet, in even these societies, the pressures for mechanized aids for all sorts of work increases daily. Percherons still pose for photographs but tractors actually pull many Old World plows.

In an even older part of the world—the so-called underdeveloped regions—the impact of technology is taking a different form. In contrast to the West, where it has added to the contentment and even the excitement of the masses, the East finds the transition from old ways to new socially and politically disturbing.

The "gadgets," from luxurious motorcars to electrical appliances, are now available to many Oriental people, but only to the upper classes and to that new pseudoaristocracy of speculators and profiteers of all shapes and sizes. Their possession of "gadgets" deepens the class lines and awakes resentments and envy.

For today's luxuries, unlike panoplied elephants of yesterday, do seem somewhat within reasonable "wanting distance" of everyone, and in fewer and fewer countries can the disappointments of the "little fellow" be charged off to imperialists.

To be sure, in the early days of the West's Industrial Revolution, concentration of power accrued to a limited number of persons, widened social gaps between them and their neighbors, and did away with many oldtime person-to-person relations in trade and the shop. But a great leveling-up has been going on ever since for multitudes in the West. The East is just beginning to face that challenge.

The problems that technology forces on the East have even more disturbing aspects in Africa. The impact of Western economic life and of the world flow of information has weakened and sometimes destroyed entirely the old tribal moral systems. New ways have provided both the means to freedom and desire for freedom from the rule of the tribal chief.

In such a transition period even the question of simple individual right and wrong seems to find no certain answers.

A leading New York preacher recently warned his congregation that "ours is a generation of mass media, mind manipulation and social engineering which gravely threatens our personal significance." Without that—a sense of his significance—the individual seeks vainly for a sense of well-being. He at least is becoming aware of the many forms of attack which would deprive him of this in an age of mechanized materialism.

All history tells us the individual can win, provided he knows there's a battle under way and that he has a significant role to play in it.

5.

In some places the battle will continue to be not a coping with luxuries but a simple achieving of subsistence—in India, for example, where on July 25, 1958, the prime minister took his two grandsons to a small village outside New Delhi to witness a novel experiment: a team of bullocks generating enough electricity to operate a woodworking factory by day and to light the entire village by night.

Prime Minister Jawaharlal Nehru belonged to a generation that had passed its childhood in the last days of the horse-

and-carriage era, that reached maturity as automobiles and airplanes began to shrink the globe, that now sees man preparing to hurtle rockets at the moon.

His grandsons, just entering adolescence, might well live to see manned space travel become a fact. What further marvels they may experience we do not know. But we may safely forecast that in their lifetime, as in that of their grandfather, the primary motive power in their country will be neither jet propulsion nor the released powers of the atom: it will be bullock power.

To say this is not to disparage India in an age that launches sputniks into space and sends forth nuclear submarines to patrol the polar ice. India, second most populous country in the world, has produced outstanding natural scientists, including a Nobel Prize winner. It already has a nuclear reactor in operation and has mapped one of the most ambitious programs to harness the atom peacefully outside the major nuclear powers.

But, in common with the underdeveloped countries of the world, India's major problem today and tomorrow is not how to jump from what Mr. Nehru has called the "cow-dung era" into the atomic age. (Cakes made from cow dung are the chief fuel of rural India.) Rather, it is how to make available to the 80 per cent of its people who do live in the cow-dung era the benefits that the Western countries consider commonplace—electricity, running water and, above all, a full stomach.

In Pakistan, Burma, Thailand, Indonesia, and across the Bamboo Curtain in North Vietnam and in Communist China, while technological changes have transformed the faces of many cities, in the villages peasants still wade knee-deep in their paddies or turn up their wheat fields as did their ancestors centuries ago. Thus, in Asia, the technological revolution must be increasingly a rural revolution. Otherwise the gap between modern city and backward village—profound even in as industrialized a country as Japan—becomes ever wider, accentuating social imbalances that lead to political overturns.

Even the Chinese Communists, who boast of their rapid industrialization and cite impressive lists of statistics on rising steel and machine production, are becoming aware of this. More and more, they are beginning to emphasize small and medium factories, instead of huge, costly industrial complexes; more and more, they are trying to bring immediate, though modest, improvements in peasant production methods instead of expensive, Soviet-modeled mechanization schemes.

It is in democratic India, however, that the most hopeful efforts along this line are going on, and the bullock-powered generator, though it was the contribution of American engineers and designers, illustrates the unique direction that this country's technological revolution is taking.

Bullock-generated electricity was an idea that came to Leigh Stevens, an American management consultant, when he toured India five years ago with an international study team on small industries. One-quarter of the world's cattle population lives in India; and Mr. Stevens noted that in the life of the village—where 80 per cent of India's people live— the bullock was indispensable.

With his team of white Brahman bulls the villager plowed his fields; with it he turned the creaking Persian wheel to bring water up from the village well to irrigate land potentially fertile but shriveled by the relentless sun.

Could not modern technology be harnessed to improve the efficiency of the Persian wheel and bring more water up within a given period? Mr. Stevens reasoned. Could it not be made to transform the uneven, lethargic movement of the bullocks into the rapid revolutions needed to generate electricity?

With the assistance of the Ford Foundation, and giving generously of his own time and resources, Mr. Stevens called on leading American companies to help him solve these problems. The Texas Gas Transmission Company developed a system of chains and sprockets to convert bullock power, moving at draw bars at less than 2 revolutions a minute, first to 20 revolutions a minute and then to 150 revolutions a minute, enough to turn a pump capable of lifting 300 gallons of water a minute. This is six times the amount of water the same bullocks, turning a traditional Persian wheel, can lift.

Next, the General Electric Company of New York helped Mr. Stevens to design a generator capable of producing power under constant pressure as bullock speed varied. Adding a belt to the system of sprockets and chains evolved for the pump, General Electric's engineers obtained 1,320 revolutions a minute—the average speed of the generator.

This bullock-powered generator can be used by day to supply enough power to run a village industry employing twenty to fifty people. This helps to solve India's pressing unemployment problem at its root—the village. At night it can light a village of 150 houses, with one 25-watt bulb in each house, and fifteen 100-watt street lamps.

Such are the dimensions of what promises to be the most important technological change in the Indian village since the invention of the Persian wheel itself. The models set up in Kranpur, the village that Mr. Nehru and his grandsons visited, are American-made—they are the gifts of the companies that developed them. But every component in these models is capable of being produced in India—and probably will be, once the present experimental stage is concluded and mass production can begin.

Like India, Communist China also boasts of developing animal-generated electricity. Peking newspapers claim that in Inner Mongolia technicians have invented a generator powered by donkeys. But since Peking, unlike India, is highly selective about admitting visitors and about allowing visitors to travel, it is not possible either to verify this claim or to test the generator's capacities.

Another recent invention claimed by Peking is a machine for transplanting rice shoots. In China and Japan, rice is sowed in seedbeds in the spring. In summer, the rice shoots are transplanted and carefully spaced. This is heavy labor, and it must be completed in as short a time as possible, in order to give rice plants a maximum growing season. Recently Peking released a photograph of a man propelling a wooden contraption by means of which six rows of rice shoots could be transplanted simultaneously. The device looks ungainly, but, if it proves efficient, it will help release tomorrow's Asian peasant from one of the most taxing of his chores.

Meanwhile, in Japan, industrially the most advanced country in Asia, with a population more than half urban, peasants are beginning to reap the fruit of improved agricultural machinery and techniques. Many peasants, especially in prosperous, crowded southwestern Honshu, use minuscule two- and three-horsepower tractors. Improved seeds, insecticides, and fertilizers have raised crop yields and this year, for the fourth year in a row, Japan expects a bumper rice harvest.

Asia's technological revolution is modest by American standards. Yet in the prospects it opens up—freedom first from want, then from drudgery, and increased opportunities to enjoy life instead of being enslaved by its mechanics—its impact on the three-fifths of mankind that dwell on the earth's largest continent is profound.

6.

Like Asia, the Middle East is picking up speed toward a future freer of material limitations. In 1958 smelting began in the first of the blast furnaces at Egypt's new Iron and Steel Works at Helwan beside the Nile south of Cairo—the first significant step in the development of heavy industry in the Arab world.

Yet within sight of the blast furnaces, Egyptian fellahin are still tilling the soil by hand, using the fass or hoe which has been the traditional implement of farmers in the Nile Valley since the time of the Pharaohs.

Industry in the Middle East for the most part, however, still means petroleum. And here again the contrasts are stark and striking. Laborers in the British Petroleum Company's big new refinery outside Aden are recruited from among tribesmen in the Aden Protectorate, who before coming down from the mountains to their new jobs wore their hair long and smeared their bodies with woad as they sallied forth on some tribal feud or vendetta.

Across the Arabian peninsula to the northeast, the great complex of Aramco, the Arabian-American Oil Company, sits side by side with a Bedouin way of life which has remained largely unchanged through the centuries.

The discovery and production of oil in vast quantities in the Middle East has brought undreamed-of wealth to an area which before had seemed condemned to poverty and stagnation—wealth which in its turn has brought both blessings and problems.

The territories where oil revenues are revolutionizing or hold out the promise of revolutionizing life are six: Kuwait, Saudi Arabia, Iraq, Bahrein, Qatar, and Iran. In some cases, governments or rulers are spending wisely the wealth so speedily and suddenly amassed. In others, it has been used selfishly and without foresight. But, without exception, the process of enrichment has been accompanied by social change of which the full consequences have yet to be measured.

Take Iraq, for example, where in the past decade oil revenues have been more sensibly and fairly spent than anywhere else in the Middle East. Since 1950, 70 per cent of the country's income from oil has gone to the Development Board, an almost autonomous organization set up to take charge of the nation's economic development program.

The board's greatest and most spectacular single achievement has been the controlling of the floodwaters of the Tigris and Euphrates, the two giant rivers of the Mesopotamian Plain. For centuries, these two rivers had burst their banks in spring and early summer, and the floods had brought disaster and destruction to the low-lying countryside. Since 1956, thanks to the work of the Development Board, this threat has been removed. The floodwaters of the Tigris and Euphrates now are diverted into lakes at Wadi Tharthar and Habbaniya—diversion schemes which have cost a total of about 70 million dollars.

What else has the Iraq Development Board done? Plenty. New roads, new bridges, new housing schemes, new schools, new hospitals, new power stations; yes, and new factories— these are all beginning to appear in Iraq. Yet these technological achievements proved inadequate to keep pace with the great social and political ferment which was all the time building up under the surface, and which eventually burst into the open with the revolution of July, 1958.

The old regime, which had had the wisdom to establish the

Development Board, had been too slow to appreciate the importance of the development of human as well as of material resources.

But despite the recent political upheaval, Iraq has brighter prospects for its economic future than any other Arab country of the Middle East. It has money—from oil. It has land. It has water. And it has no pressing population problem. How much more difficult to solve must seem the economic problems of a have-not country like Egypt! It has not enough money. It has not enough land. It has not enough water. And all the time its already overcrowded population is increasing at the alarming rate of more than fifty every hour.

Land and water resources in the Nile Valley are so restricted that it is to straightforward industrialization that the Nasser regime looks to provide employment for the country's teeming millions and to increase the national wealth. For a number of years there have been the great textile mills at Mehalla el-Kubra and Kafr el-Zayat in the Nile Delta. The new Iron and Steel Works at Helwan have recently started production. A new fertilizer factory at Aswan is to be completed in 1960.

But even in Egypt—though a have-not, yet in some ways the most developed of all the Arab lands—the handicaps are formidable. Skills are still lacking for operating the most modern technical and industrial equipment. Capital is hard to come by. The climate is not conducive to a good day's work. Communications need to be improved. And the country's fuel and power resources are still limited.

For reasons such as these, many in the Middle East pin their hope to some revolutionary invention or technological development which might open the door to a better standard of living for the millions in the Arab world who hitherto have known only squalor and poverty. Perhaps, for example, men might soon discover some way to use nuclear or even solar energy to distill sea water cheaply.

A research program in Israel has perfected trapping devices which harness about 90 per cent of available sunlight. But the storage of this energy still is done by physical means, such as heating large tanks of water, and this heat is quickly dissipated.

If the storage problem is solved, solar energy could become efficiently usable for heating and cooling buildings. In the meantime, researchers in various countries are trying to tap the sun for such ultimate purposes as changing brackish water to fresh, powering space equipment, and improving food yields.

The men who are doing this research are not always too pleased with the expectant kibitzing that goes on while they experiment. As one of them, Dr. Daniel I. Arnon, of the University of California, says: "Our basic philosophy is that knowledge comes first. Atomic energy was discovered because scientists tried to understand the atom rather than seeking to make bombs or produce usable atomic energy. . . . The new weed killers came out of research to determine what makes a plant grow."

But most of the pure researchers are aware of what their applied science colleagues are hoping for. Palmer Putnam explains the prize at one point in his book *Energy in the Future* (Van Nostrand):

"If we should convert to man's use 10 per cent of the solar energy falling on land at an efficiency of 10 per cent—not an impossibility—then we find that we could supply the light, heat, power, and nutrient for 17 billion people."

7.

Not only the underdeveloped countries will need new resources for meeting the future's demand for food. In the United States, today's farmer feeds himself and twenty other people, in contrast with the farmer of 1904, who fed only himself and seven others. But as population explodes, the farmer will have to do better.

Solar energy is one of the advances that can help him. He also looks toward—

Discoveries in biological science—possibly even solution of the mystery of photosynthesis, which would probably "revolutionize methods of food production and allow us to feed almost unlimited numbers," according to one expert.

Increased use of irrigation, possibly augmented by sea water if sufficiently economic freshening methods are eventually devised.

Control of agricultural environment, including possibly, but not certainly, the weather.

Finally, and perhaps most provocative of all, the as yet undeveloped possibilities of atomic science as applied to agriculture. Already substantial experiments are under way to harness atomic knowhow for farmers, but the ultimate belongs to the future.

Meanwhile, farmers progress on the basis of achievements of the past fifty years such as—

Increasing knowledge of genetics and development of hybrid crops (notably, hybrid corn) and animals, increasing both quality and quantity.

Development of crops new to the United States, such as

soybeans, which today provide more than 50 per cent of the protein used in nutritionally balanced food for livestock and poultry, grown now on 21 million acres and valued at a billion dollars. With this trend to new crops must be coupled development of new uses for traditional crops.

Synthetic fixation of nitrogen which has given farmers fertilizer in economic abundance and accounts in great degree for the land's astounding increase in productivity.

Genetic control of disease resistance in plants; development of pesticides; new safeguards to animal health.

Automation, which is revolutionizing production of poultry and is being applied experimentally to larger meat animals and some dairy operations.

Irrigation in new areas.

Improved soil conservation practices.

Refinement of processing and marketing procedures which give consumers "built-in maid service"—foods canned, cooked, frozen, or otherwise processed to save consumers' time.

Tomorrow's agriculture will probably continue to be influenced by three major factors, each of which has played a role not yet fully assessed in bringing agriculture to its present position.

The land-grant colleges, with their broad educational mission and their system of research and experiment stations, extension service, county agents, and home demonstration workers; private industry, with its ambitious research, development and marketing projects; and the federal government, which has assumed a degree of management and support of farm affairs unknown to previous generations—and which pursues an extensive research program of its own.

As better uses of the sun and the land are explored, the

sea also invites research. It is a source not only of food but also of minerals.

Taking minerals from the land is like living on your savings. But mining the sea is living on income.

That is why many scientists look to the oceans to meet the fast-growing mineral needs of mankind.

At the moment only bromine, iodine, magnesium, potash, and, of course, table salt are extracted from sea water in quantity. But the 320 million cubic miles of earth's oceans are a great reservoir of many other critical materials which await only the incentive of economic necessity and the key of advanced technology to become available to mankind.

The chief problem with this reservoir is dilution. Its wealth is thinly spread so it is in no sense a "rich ore." But this dilution is compensated by the ease of handling large quantities of water and the fact that minerals taken from the oceans are renewed year by year. These are advantages no land mine can claim.

Every stream and river reaching the sea carries with it dissolved minerals. Some of these are taken directly from rocks and soil. Some come secondhand from man.

Metals corroding in junk yards are slowly converted to other forms through the action of wind, rain, and chemical change, and eventually find their way into the water flowing seaward. Rich phosphate fertilizers, mined from rock and spread on farm lands, likewise go through a long series of steps to end up in the ocean reservoir.

Many of the materials could be extracted today if the process could be made to pay. But economics are against it. There is the famous example of gold, present in sea water to the extent of 25 tons per cubic mile. That is a lot of gold. Yet the concentration is so thin all processes devised for extracting the metal have cost more than the gold recovered is worth.

Solar evaporation uses mankind's cheapest fuel—sunlight—but it is a primitive and land-consuming way of extracting sea salts in quantity. Thus, scientists are looking for chemical and electrochemical means of extraction that, while they use more expensive fuels, will still be economical.

Using chemical means rather than evaporation to mine the sea is essentially the difference between removing large amounts of water from the salts and removing only the materials wanted from large amounts of water. Here is a challenging frontier of research that tackles the dilution problem head on.

Crossing this frontier, as well as many others in the march against material limitations, depends to a considerable extent on economics. Even though ours will be a world of increased push-button ease, industrial automation, and distributive competency, it cannot be a Utopia. Its progress and its wealth must always rest on its productivity. We cannot expect to take more out of our system than we put into it. Our machines will increase individual productivity. Our transit and distribution systems will multiply it. But productivity there must be.

This means that serious voids in economic knowledge which exist today must be wiped out. We have it within our own hands to control extremes of economic deviation. We need not go from boom to boom, dented with periodic unemployment and recession.

But to escape this recurrence, sometimes called "the business cycle," we shall need to know that cyclical boom and cyclical bust are only the result of excessive behavior on the part of consumers, industries, and government.

The more our schools teach students the fundamentals of productivity, market research, distribution, and inventory control, the sooner shall we master our economic ignorance.

In the competitive world market place, the industry which

cannot rest secure on a productivity system will be wiped out, and the union members engaged in it will become jobless.

What is productivity? It is an old-fashioned, outmoded economic term for the output per individual worker hour. Here in the United States we have maintained an average increase each year of 2 to 3 per cent in our productivity. As we have added machines to our system, we have stepped up worker productivity.

Automation and machines will progressively step up productivity in the years ahead. But we must pay careful attention, as our commitments increase, that we keep this stepping-up process vital.

Should we be content with a mere 2 per cent gain a year? The answer seems clearly to be in the negative. This cannot do the job required by the growing population in the United States and the needs of the underdeveloped nations.

A productivity increase of 4 to 5 per cent each year is the least we should settle for. The Rockefeller report in 1958 called for at least 5 per cent. This is a reasonable expectation of our technological society. We as a people should expect it. But we should understand it before world competition forces us to understand it in a painful way.

Should we lose this vital awareness of productivity, this key to our success and that of a greater world community, we then face the problem of running in a continual straight line of no progress and stagnation, and eventually into economic fossilization.

It is possible that, as more of our citizens become sensitive to the need for better citizen control of the question of productivity, of wages, of profits, of prices, of taxes, we shall do as is done in Scandinavia—insist on the "third man's right," the right of the consumer to be represented when division of the fruits of productivity between management, labor, and government is made.

Our progress, too, depends on an improved knowledge in our government of the uses of debt, monetary powers, credit, and taxation as methods of providing the kind of economic atmosphere which will keep our nation viable and able to participate in the fast-knitting world community. We face a serious risk of overtaxing in our economy and in this way stifling our growth.

These matters require alert citizenship and a ready willingness on the part of our schools to teach these fundamentals of our economy. We have left the world of *laissez faire* (let nature take its course) in economic affairs far behind. Even though we still suffer from encrustations of *laissez faire* in our present economic system, the growing competition of the world and the growing demands of our own people and of those millions in other lands will force us to scrape these off.

The future is big. It can go up and up. It could go in a straight line into stagnation. It could turn down into fossilization. It's up to us.

8.

From a European point of view, the pattern of the future can be symbolized by three such familiar everyday instances of change as the car, the television, and the school. Through these symbols it can be seen that, although material progress promises to be great, the new era that is dawning in Europe does not belong to things. It belongs to people.

The keynote is going to be freedom. Our freedoms will grow and multiply, rooted in a better sense of personal responsibility. The demands of technological development insist upon this. Reaction against it by forces opposed to freedom may be violent but cannot halt the trend.

The car is most often presented in the literature of our day as the symbol of prestige, power, conformity and, sometimes, debt; and the television as the symbol of inertia or futility. (Only the school gets good marks all round.)

But also they can all be the symbols of widening horizons.

The car, after all, is the product of what is undoubtedly going to be Europe's key industry. And in this context it also stands for all those other products that in a rapidly expanding industrial system are going to relieve millions upon millions from unnecessary drudgery.

But the car is also a mechanical extension to personal freedom. It makes one independent. It increases the range of travel; it breaks the tyranny of the timetable. It rides over boundaries and shatters them.

Television, besides representing a whole new industry of electronic marvels only at the beginning of the beginning of development, is a symbol of our growing awareness of one another. We know what is going on. The foreign, the distant, the unaccustomed—here they are now in our living rooms.

The quality of this awareness is surely going to be improved by the extended education that is itself imperative to further technological growth.

These three trends in turn seem to make the eventual unity of Europe certain, despite alarms and hesitations. Technological growth demands unity. It is bound to come whether or not that unity is ever formalized in a federation.

The three trends also point to a revolution in the organization and administration of industry, changing the concept of the roles of management and labor. They must upgrade "the worker" and probably will eliminate "the boss." For we shall eventually be very close to equality of training and education, and will then have to make a reality of the teamwork.

Furthermore, our three trends, the widening and improving of the range of human awareness, plus the fact of rapid technological development itself, are likely to have a profound effect on government. Authoritarian government, at least as we have known it in various countries in the past, may indeed become a sheer impossibility.

Let us return to the automobile for a moment. The West European car industry has doubled in size since 1950. There is no reason why it should not double itself again.

Between 1950 and 1955 the number of cars, buses, and trucks on the roads of Europe increased by 75 per cent. Increase of 50 per cent more is estimated by 1960. This means there was an increase of 7 million vehicles in those first five years and will likely mean an increase of 9 million in the second.

Look beyond 1960 into the years ahead—eighteen years or twenty-eight years or thirty-eight years—and can one then doubt that the car will change even the very look of Europe, causing new cities to arise and ancient cities to be at once restored and renewed?

Already West Germany's ten-year program envisages the spending of 8 billion dollars on roads alone.

To power its industries Western Europe will probably spend an extra 150 billion dollars before 1975, an increasing proportion of it on nuclear power.

By 1975 there may quite well be one hundred nuclear power stations working in Europe.

It is even possible—a Jules Verne would not hesitate to say it was inevitable—that before 1975, Europe will have unlocked the secret of inexhaustible power from the cheapest source imaginable, sea water.

That is the promise of the experiments with thermonuclear apparatus, like Britain's Zeta, which are currently going ahead well in half a dozen countries.

Such resources of power, unlimited by geography or geology, will provide Europe with its chance to solve finally the intractable problem of its own underdeveloped areas. Where there is no power, as in southern Italy, or remote Greece, Europe will provide power. Where the soil is poor, it can be enriched.

These areas will need capital development on a vast scale. But they need also customers.

For buying is just as important as selling. Which is the reason the fashion of describing a commercial society as "acquisitive," founded on the expression of greed, has served us badly. One's riches do not depend on others being poor, as we have been told.

Indeed, in a commercial society they depend on others being increasingly well off. And it works both ways. It is to the advantage of others if you also become increasingly well off. You're the customer.

In only five years the increase in Europeans' buying in the stores and supermarkets is expected to amount to 25 billion dollars. Europeans will probably be spending half of this extra money on household goods, electrical gadgets, cars, and clothing.

In recent years gross investment has been running at 20 per cent of national income. One-half of this has been spent on new machinery and plant to boost production still further.

We can thus expect very high rates of productivity growth. Combined with this will be the revolutions of electronics and of automation and combined with them the development of a single European market.

What does this mean? It means the imperative extension of education. Children will stay at school longer. Millions more will get technical training. Management will need to be more enterprising as well as better informed. Employees may have to be prepared to switch jobs and learn new skills. The new jobs may be in what was yesterday a different country. Everywhere the accent is to be on learning.

Now Europeans have to give meaning to an incredible, fantastic, technological revolution. And doing that will provide them with a new revolution.

9.

Underlying the world's technological progress—and the challenges it presents—are the achievements of natural science. The level where natural scientists are facing the unknown is the level of basic research and not of technological development. A nation could enjoy a good bit of modern technology without ever indulging in basic scientific research or being touched by its ethic. But it would be imported technology.

On the other hand, it can be argued that any nation that wants to build up its own technological strength and not be dependent on foreign specialists must devote some of its efforts to basic research.

Engineering development takes its raw material from the general pool of human knowledge. But it does not contribute to that pool. As far as science and engineering are concerned, basic research is the fountainhead.

If a nation is to have strong engineering development capabilities of its own, which it needs to be a modern industrial country, if it is not merely to borrow the technology of others, it must have at least a few scientists intimately acquainted with the general pool of knowledge.

Modern natural science is more than splitting atoms, exploring ocean depths, or launching earth-girdling satellites. It is a great mental adventure that has become one of the driving forces of Western civilization.

Its achievements in the material world are only the outward evidence of the mental dominion that has made these possible.

By rejecting dogma in favor of testing concepts by their fidelity to observed fact, natural science gave men a new standard of truth. It has shown them how to throw off the slough of mysticism and to embrace the universe in their understanding.

Harvard University's Nobel Prize-winning physicist Percy Bridgman has called the rise of natural science "primarily a development of effective intelligence." He has also defined the "scientific method" as simply doing one's best with one's mind, no holds barred.

This basic ethic, this commitment to truth and to intelligent thinking, has been natural science's principal contribution to Western civilization. It is anathema to racial, religious, or other blindly held prejudices. It is the declaration of man's independence from occultism. It has added a new dimension to human dignity.

In their own special field of studying the physical universe, scientists have found this commitment an essential prerequisite to success in their search for understanding. But, in overthrowing long-held dogmas in their own field, they also helped establish the primacy of unfettered intelligence, intelligence harnessed only to truth, in all areas of thinking.

"Science," says the British scientist and philosopher Jacob Bronowski, "is the creation of concepts and their exploration in the facts. It has no other test of the concept than its empirical truth to fact."

This authority "of experienced fact as a face of truth," he adds, has been "the mainspring which has moved our civilization since the Renaissance." (*Science and Human Values,* Julian Messner, Inc.)

This fundamental commitment of natural science is often forgotten in the race to squeeze practical benefits from our prolific research laboratories. But the commitment remains an effective leaven in the thinking of man nonetheless, for nations cannot accept the fruits of natural science without imbibing some of the thinking that underlies it.

A simple historical example illustrates how revolutionary that thinking has been and continues to be.

The ancient Greek philosopher Aristotle maintained that heavy bodies have an inherent tendency to fall and light bodies to rise. He said that air had a tendency to rise and consequently was weightless.

For centuries, Aristotle's doctrine was accepted without question. It seemed simple common sense. Then Galileo set about showing how misleading such common sense can be.

He found a means of weighing air by balancing an inflated pig's bladder against the weight of a container of water. He let the air escape by puncturing the bladder and the pan holding the water sank. This proved that air has weight.

Galileo and other such Renaissance scientists refuted many dogmatic teachings in this way. Each time their technique was one of reasoning from careful observation and definitive experiments.

The authority "of experienced fact as a face of truth" had emerged as a force in human thinking. It was to make all the difference between the constricting forces of superstition, dogma, and mysticism and the growing dominion of men as thinkers.

To quote the historian, Rudolf Thiel, these early scientists showed that "appearances are deceptive in both astronomy and physics. . . . The conclusion that the laws of nature are not obvious, cannot be fathomed by mere reasoning, was . . . fraught with consequences. . . . Once it was accepted, the old way of philosophizing was discredited. Once it was accepted, Western man began his investigation and conquest of nature." (*And There Was Light,* Knopf.)

Today men everywhere seem eager to share in this investigation and conquest. It is obvious they will have to accept the mental consequences as well as the practical benefits. The discipline of testing concepts against the facts will not leave national or personal prejudices untouched in the long run.

Indeed, some Western scientists have seen this as a reason for hope in a politically tense world. They see the thought force of natural science bringing a more rational and tolerant outlook to all nations and eventually reducing international tensions.

There are so many conflicting factors at work that it is impossible to say whether this hope is more than wishful thinking. On the other hand, scientific thinking cannot help having a profound effect on non-Western peoples, especially those who traditionally have looked at the natural universe through the lens of mysticism.

In this connection, it should be pointed out that the ethic of natural science is not like a moral code that men conveniently can put aside when they want to. At the crucial level where a scientist is face to face with the unknown, the penalty for failing to observe the "morality" of research is total. You can't cheat nature into revealing her secrets. You have to play by the rules or fail.

In Western society, traditional religion felt the impact of this commitment centuries ago and it has been warring with natural science ever since. One of the charges frequently hurled is that scientists have thrown God out of His universe.

It is, of course, true that scientists study material nature. But they are under no commitment to materialism. They

have thrown traditional limiting concepts of God and life out
the window. But their search for underlying principle unfettered by human preconceptions and their insistence on
man's individual right to seek truth honestly for himself
bespeak a humility foreign to dogmatic religious thinking.

There is a profound difference between the search for
truth based upon concepts that are held merely by faith or
authority, or by the appearance of being self-evident, and the
liberating discipline that puts no human concept beyond
the test of matching its consequences with fact.

There is much more at stake in this difference than the
control of our material environment. Dr. Bronowski notes
significantly that "when we discard the test of fact in what a
star is, we discard it in what a man is. A society holds together
by the respect man gives to man; it fails, in fact it falls apart
into groups of fear and power, when its concept of man is
false."

This is why the consequences of the scientific approach to
truth have reached so far beyond the laboratory in Western
nations. As this approach spreads to the rest of the world,
one wonders what will be its larger consequences for all
mankind.

A century ago, scientists were confident they had taken
the measure of the universe and could explain all significant
phenomena, including life, in mechanical and chemical terms,
with the concept of evolution thrown in. The universe and
man were considered smoothly running mechanisms, basically analogous to the planets whirling with mathematical
precision in their orbits and the intricate near perfection of
the watchmaker's art.

Matter was considered substantial and solid in its very
essence. It was thought to be composed of billiard ball-like
atoms, indescribably small but concrete and indivisible.

Except for a few gaps here and there, knowledge of this matter was considered basically complete. Given the state, forces, and motions of all the atoms and masses in the universe at any one moment, scientists believed they could, in theory at least, forecast the course of that universe forever after. No other principle than the material laws then formulated was considered necessary.

This overconfident materialism first faltered and then dissolved under the impact of new discoveries whose meaning it was incompetent to fathom.

Today, the physicist has thirty fundamental particles with which to explain material phenomena. Any day, he may discover more. But these are what he has at the moment, and they are a far cry from the nugget-hard atoms of the nineteenth century.

Constantly disappearing in a burst of radiation or emerging from formless energy, these particles build up stable forms of matter only through their interaction with one another. The rules governing the particles and their interaction are only beginning to take shape from the great mass of data physicists have been accumulating.

It has been the physicist's faith that he eventually will be able to explain the material world in terms of a few fundamental particles governed by simple rules—a sort of cosmic chess game. But while physicists still hold to this faith, it is being challenged by the unsolved riddle of the particles.

J. Robert Oppenheimer summed this up in a *Saturday Evening Post* article by saying: "In particle physics we may have to accept an arbitrary, complicated, not very orderly set of facts, without seeing behind them the harmony in terms of which they might be understood. It is the special faith and dedication of our profession that we will not lightly concede such a defeat."

The nineteenth century would not have understood such a statement.

Speaking of this century, Dr. Werner Heisenberg, one of the founders of modern atomic theory, has observed:

Confidence in the scientific method and in rational thinking replaced all other safeguards of the human mind.... The most important change brought about by [modern physics] consists in the dissolution of this rigid frame of concepts....

The lesson of modern physics has again opened scientists' thinking to the value of other approaches to other areas of knowledge, approaches that use terms—mind, love, and God—which to physicists are vaguely defined. To quote Dr. Heisenberg, concepts such as these have grown out of the long experience of mankind, are part of mankind's "natural language," and have "immediate contact with reality."

Thus, it is worth while to remember that the natural science that is giving men dominion over their environment is only part of the story, only one face of the challenge.

The moral, ethical, and social forces of the world, indeed the spiritual nature of man himself, need to be equally thoroughly studied and understood, and the knowledge thus gained needs to be constructively applied, if mankind's full freedom from material limitations is to be realized.

MAN'S RELATION TO MAN

Freedom for Spiritual Unfoldment

1.

MAN'S GREAT FUTURE PROMISES NOT ONLY INCREASED FREEDOM from material limitations but increased freedom for spiritual unfoldment. The latter advance is less tangible but no less inevitable in view of the progress already achieved. It will continue unless men, while breaking the chains of matter, ironically put on the chains of materialism.

Where are the signs of the expanding freedom for spiritual unfoldment? They appear strikingly in man's relation to man —in the family, the school, the church, the town, the nation, the world. They are hinted in the awareness of the writer, the creativity of the artist. They are focused ultimately in the individual, in the moral sensitivity that has grown in man's thinking through the ages.

This is another story that begins at home.

It will be great to go to the moon. But earth never invented anything better than coming home—provided home is a center of affection where parents love each other and their children intelligently, and where children admire and respect their parents and want to grow up to be like them.

What is the status of family life in the United States?

"The home is now subject to the greatest strain to which

it has been subjected in all of its history. All sorts of forces seem to conspire to wreck this foundation-stone of our civilization. . . .

"The multiplication of machinery seems to have a tendency to break it down. . . . The cost of living is constantly increasing and in order to meet household expenses it seems necessary for women to become wage-earners.

"In the old days, father, mother, and children all worked under the same roof. Now all are scattered during the day."

Sound familiar? Those paragraphs are not clipped from yesterday's newspaper but from the second issue of *The Christian Science Monitor,* dated November 27, 1908.

Yet fifty years later the family is somehow still afloat, showing many signs of stress but also flying hopeful pennants of healthy progress.

In a sea of variables, the one constant has been two facts: Parents still love their children and children still love and glorify their parents.

Among the welter of changes since 1900, three stand out: (1) Today, the family clan, like the atom, is split. All that's left are mother, dad, and the youngsters. (2) Living is no longer "naturally" done; it's downright deliberate. (3) It's harder to be a good parent today than ever, and much more confusing.

Clarence Day's *Life with Father* has indelibly stamped upon us the picture of the Victorian era—Father Day the general, Mother Day the lieutenant, and the children lowly privates.

There were no pesky questions in anybody's mind of how children should behave. They should speak when spoken to, be seen but rarely heard. The switch solved most problems.

Home for breakfast, lunch, and dinner, father was never far

from home. He managed the money, made the decisions, and boomed out the family law.

Grandparents were in the home. Uncles and aunts were neighbors, and cousins were counted by dozens. Life had an accustomed routine.

On farms, where two-thirds of the population lived, members depended on each other for survival. A child was not another mouth to feed but an economic asset—two more hands to do the chores. Parents and children lived close. The family was the center of learning, companionship, work, and play.

But behold the current model of the Day family. Interdependence to a large extent is gone. The family seems largely stripped of many of its traditional functions.

Daddy Day has lost status as the sole breadwinner and authoritarian head. He is more the leader of a democratic group. This is the century of children. Children's rights have been recognized. Their emotional well-being is a major concern.

Mommy has zoomed in stature, contributing to the family income or earning all of it. She chauffeurs, pays the bills, and spends most of the money. With dad traveling or commuting to suburbia, she makes most of the decisions about the children.

And children are expensive. Hence there are fewer of them per family. Only recently have families again begun to grow.

And whom do we see sitting in the living room of an evening? Grandma? Grandpa? Auntie? No, indeed, they are far away, for the Days have moved many times. Following the job, their home has become a rolling stone. No, in that chair is the baby sitter, an important figure of the twentieth century.

Teen-ager Teddy Day can earn up to $600 a summer.

When Dad decrees: "No, you can't have that new sports coat," Teddy says to himself: "Fiddle, I'll buy it myself."

With economic independence growing, Mr. and Mrs. Day find they cannot get respect just by noisily demanding it. They have honestly to earn it. Their major parental role today is guiding their children, planning for their education, and interpreting a complex world.

Today a family's income is not secure. Mr. and Mrs. Day live under the universal economic threat of "produce or you're expendable." In addition to that pressure, they have to work hard at being parents.

Being wise, the Days use the station wagon to unite their family instead of split it. They take vacations together, go camping and ski in winter. They take color slides to enjoy later. They know family unity these days doesn't happen. It has to be planned.

With so many mothers working and with divorces so easy to get, the Days know that today as never before the bond of affectionate love is the only thing that holds them together. So when the going is rough, they seek professional counseling.

Do social workers tell them punitively as they used to: "You've been bad. We'll decide what's best for you"? They do not. A new faith in the basic goodness of man and his ability to work out his problems causes counselors to do things with, not to or for, their clients.

Their advice is sounder than ever. For instance: "The true motive for marriage is giving, not getting"; "Strive for wholesome feelings for your children"; "If you really want to keep your children, you have to let them go."

With such help the Days work out their problems.

Not all American families are like the Days, past or present. Family life, riding the pendulum of society itself, tends to swing from one extreme to another.

But most families, moving forward gradually, find themselves at some point of progression between the old and new modes of life. Occupying this middle ground, they help keep family behavior from moving too far in either direction.

2.

The family, however, is not the only influence on young people. From home it is just a hop, skip, and a bus ride to school.

Place: Any American town on a sparkling autumn morning. Along the main street and down every side street come troops of children, the younger ones skipping and tripping as they gaily talk to each other, the teen-agers in purposeful small groups, carrying stacks of books. Around the corners come the big yellow school buses and strings of private automobiles filled with children. Intermingled with all this is the bicycle brigade.

All are given the stop or go sign by a regular traffic policeman who greets many a boy and girl with friendly banter, or more often by a young woman in policeman's uniform—a mother serving on the force twice a day at school crossings.

These children are the nation's stake in the future. They are headed for the big buildings with the wide windows and the generous playing fields in various parts of the town. It is a daily event in the life of the vast free public school system built up to pass along to each younger generation the cultural heritage felt to be fundamental and vital. It is a symbol of man's concern for the education of youth in the countries of the Western world.

Children of these Western countries are comparatively well taken care of as to schooling. The vast majority have a chance to go to school during childhood years—indeed, are required to—and the trend has been to push up the school leaving age, insuring the young person educational opportunities up to the age of fifteen and sixteen, and making provision for continuation or evening schools for the young working person.

In the more prosperous lands young people stay in school longer. In the wealthy United States a high proportion finish secondary school and go on into some form of higher education. More and more the adult population is seeking to strengthen this trend. Free public education for all is the goal.

This, in essence, is a spiritual aim. It is more than a mere effort to make the coming generation conform to the adult pattern of each land. It is more than an effort to advance society by training leaders in certain needed fields as is done in totalitarian countries.

In the free countries of the Western world, two deeply spiritual ideals have guided governments and adult citizens in almost every development that has taken place in education in the past fifty years.

The first is to provide equal educational opportunity for all. The second is to give the individual every possible opportunity for unfoldment. Every development in education of the last fifty years in free countries of the Western world finds its inspiration in one or the other of these goals.

Equality or educational opportunity does not mean identical schooling for all. It could mean this if all young people needed exactly the same kind of education. But of course they don't. It does mean, though, that all children should have the same chance to go to school. Therefore, compulsory education laws see to it that parents don't put them to work at an early age. It means, too, that as they grow older, if they must work, there are free night schools, adult education courses, the wonderful folk high schools of Scandinavia.

When some children failed or tended to drop out of school

because the traditional pattern designed for the bookminded did not open up equal educational opportunity for them, practical and vocational courses were added, and the comprehensive high school developed—especially in the United States, but now spreading beyond its borders.

The ideal of providing equality of opportunity, combined with a concern to give the individual a chance to make the most of his possibilities, has spurred the development of scholarships at several levels. Children and young people "must not be deprived for lack of funds." The British "public" schools like Harrow and Eton have used this modern way to maintain their original aims of providing education to topnotch youngsters. Scholarships for college students and gifts to schools and colleges by businesses and foundations are inspired by this same idealism.

An urgent concern for the individual and his contribution to society has given birth to the child-study movement that has done much to change classroom teaching. The initial reaction against what now seems an overemphasis in the schools to demand conformity in children was the muchmaligned "progressive education movement" growing out of the teachings of the 1920's of educators, such as John Dewey. It emphasized studying the child's needs, brightening up the teaching of all subjects, making them seem more urgent to children, and gave greater attention to the individual's possibilities and to adapting approaches that would bring them out.

The excesses that aroused intense opposition did not prevent the widespread and lasting contributions made by this movement on both sides of the Atlantic and in many parts of the world. As the half-century went forward, classrooms, especially in elementary schools, became quite different places—more informal, homelike, flexible, with children serving on self-governing committees, carrying on discussions, planning school trips, and no longer sitting all day in stiff rows of screwed-down desks.

With all the children of all the people coming to school, and a growing social consciousness, as cities mushroomed in size and urban problems knocked at school doors, teachers found out that Johnny or Mary had had no breakfast, or that their lunch boxes were pretty slim. So the government-sponsored school lunch movement began. With the need for providing many different kinds of education, the small neighborhood or rural school seemed inadequate, and school districts were enlarged. The consolidated school took form.

With larger classes and less intimate knowledge of the child by the teacher, the need of trained guidance work was seen, and is a movement growing slowly but steadily. Parents no longer lived a few blocks from school. They needed to be brought in to confer and to help, and the parent-teacher movement grew up.

What a different school world from those simple town and village days of 1908! Junior high schools were unheard of except in a few centers where they were an entirely new idea of school organization. Children walked to and from school on crisp autumn days, scuffing bright leaves, and at recess played tag and hopscotch in the school yard—minus swings and slides. The McGuffey tradition of moral teaching was still strong. "Waste Not, Want Not" was a story learned by heart.

The goal of reading was to stand besides one's desk and read out loud, no matter if one word were seen at a time and the meaning not too clear. Friday speech days brought "recitations" of Tennyson or Longfellow, and commencement meant a long series of student "orations" on erudite subjects.

It was a pleasant, simple world, untroubled by the Soviets

surpassing everyone in producing scientists, and the anxiety
of teen-agers over merit scholarship examinations and college
boards.

But who would go back? With all their recognized faults,
the schools of the Western nations have never been so good,
done such a tremendous job to meet the needs of a complex
world and a diverse population. Two world wars showed up
certain deficiencies, but also showed up a youth that faced
its challenges magnificently. Reading, mathematics—in spite
of the critics—is better taught. The study of the sciences is
being stepped up and improved. Children are longer in
school, have many more opportunities for study, for travel,
for interchange with students of all ages in other countries.
Thousands today knock at the doors of the colleges who once
would not have thought it within their reach. Cultural interests blossom into international children's art exchanges,
all-state orchestras and bands, tours to museums, book fairs.

Today, in the United States, integration of the races is raising an enormously complex challenge to the school systems
of the southern states. Quite apart from this, citizens still
criticize their schools and read books claiming that all the
basic subjects are badly taught, but this has been the pattern
for far more than fifty years. Today such criticism is increasingly welcomed, for it is seen as evidence of an active
interest, and it helps more alert educators and parents to
evaluate what the schools are doing and to work toward a
better informed public.

Schools are precious in lands where they are still scarce.
One of the most heartening developments of this half-century
is the increasing spread of free public education in lands that
have not had it until now. Providing equality of educational
opportunity, giving each individual every possible chance to

make the most of himself and to contribute to the welfare of society—these are goals mankind has for its children and youth.

3.

From the school to the church is but another step. As the individual seeks spiritual guidance for the future in the denomination of his choice, many churches look toward greater unity.

Bold steps forward in Christian cooperation were taken by Protestant churches in the United States fifty years ago with the formation in December, 1908, of the Federal Council of the Churches of Christ in America.

This move, which eventually was to be felt around the world, did not come overnight. It represented years of the church's deep longing for Christian unity. Always before, this desire had been evidenced in various ways by individual religious leaders.

The former American Evangelical Alliance, initiated in 1867, represented interested individuals from the various denominations. The Federal Council, however, was an advance over this group because it was organized by official sanction of the church.

In the year 1905, when American church groups met to draw up a constitution for the New Federal Council, French Protestants also were seeking a united voice by the founding of the Protestant Federation of France.

By the time the French council was three years old, the constitution of the new American group had been adopted by the constituent church bodies and the Federal Council became official in 1908.

So significant was this organization that it was the pattern for the World Council of Churches, which came into being in Amsterdam, in 1948. One Christian historian gives the American council credit for having "initiated the greatest experiment yet made in cooperation between churches."

Fifty years ago, when the thirty Protestant denominations in the Federal Council united in service, with a New York headquarters, the event was front-page news in *The Christian Science Monitor*, then but a fledgling newspaper in its twelfth day of publication.

Evidence that the church was beginning to feel a responsibility for the social order was mirrored in the *Monitor* account from the Philadelphia assemblage on December 7, 1908. It stated that the "three important subjects" up for discussion were "temperance, divorce, and race suicide."

At a time when the "dry" movement of the late nineteenth century was again returning to popularity, the Federal Council's committee on temperance was urging "the absolute prohibition of saloons and the abolition of the liquor traffic."

During the fifty years since the council's committee first stoutly condemned the evils of the liquor traffic, the problem of beverage alcohol has grown to such proportions that the churches in February, 1958, again came out with one of the strongest statements the council ever has made regarding alcohol.

This time, however, it was more than the organizations in the old Federal Council which were doing the speaking. In 1950, this latter group, together with seven other bodies, formed the National Council of the Churches of Christ in the U.S.A.

This body now represents thirty-four churches with 37,-870,000 members. It is associated with more than nine hundred state and local councils and two thousand ministerial associations.

The 1958 declaration on "The Churches and Alcohol" is a contrast to the issues fifty years ago. Emphasis has shifted from the 1908 call for abolition of the liquor traffic to concern about the problems of alcoholism, the church's attitude toward the alcoholic, and aspects of alcohol education which the churches should undertake.

The National Council was formed by the merging with the Federal Council of the following specialized agencies: the Foreign Missions Conference of North America, the Homes Missions Council of North America, the International Council of Religious Education, the National Protestant Council of Higher Education, the Missionary Education Movement of the United States and Canada, the United Stewardship Council, and the United Council of Church Women.

Religious leaders who have followed the trend toward greater cooperation among Christian churches point out that the whole so-called ecumenical movement—the move toward church unity— has developed in the past fifty years.

Most of the various streams of interest leading to Christian unity in the United States and other countries seem to have come to focus in larger movements since 1908.

One line is represented by the World Missionary Conference held in Edinburgh in 1910. In the mission field almost more than anywhere else, the "absurdity of a divided church" was early dramatized and the great need for unity was seen to be practically imperative.

In the nineteenth century, Europe and the United States sponsored expansion of Christianity through the mission field, but it was a divided church which was expanded. Encounter with the non-Christian world demonstrated to the various mission groups how absurd their divisions were. To become a Christian was a major accomplishment but for a convert furthermore to consider himself a Baptist, Methodist, or one of the many other Protestant faiths was almost asking too much.

The missionary conference at Edinburgh thus high-lighted the need for Christian unity. Back in the United States, individuals fired with this vision helped supply the needed impetus and within the year several denominations had established commissions on Christian unity.

This stream of interest initiated at Edinburgh crystallized in what has become known as the Faith and Order Movement. The latter's first world conference did not convene until 1927 in Lausanne, Switzerland. World War I set the churches back in their examination of each other's "historical, liturgical, and doctrinal differences" considered basic in pressing forward to organic unity.

In the meantime, the concept of the responsibility of the church for society gradually was taking shape. Critics of revivalism, which was beginning to decline in the latter half of the nineteenth century, urged a gradual "growing up" within the church, rather than sudden—sometimes prostrating—conversions. Furthermore, a social gospel was needed for the church to cope with the problems imposed by the industrial city—problems equally as challenging as those revivalism had met in the westward movement.

This concern for the social order found expression in the Life and Work Movement, which held its first world conference in Stockholm in 1925.

Both of these two latter movements have continued to grow and were incorporated in the World Council of Churches when it was formed in 1948. National mission groups, represented by the International Missionary Council, however, have only been in association with the WCC as a sister organization.

At the assembly of the IMC held in Ghana, in 1958, the world mission groups voted to merge with the WCC. The union is to be made formal in 1961.

It is as if the hearts of religious leaders during the past fifty years were being made ready for Christian unity. In 1957, many Christian churches in North America cooperated in launching one of the most ambitious projects in ecumenical history by posing the study question: "What is the nature of the unity we seek?" The study was climaxed by the first North American Faith and Order Study Conference held in Oberlin, Ohio, September, 1957.

4.

The home, the school, the church are centers but not circumferences for family life as it moves into the future. The individual reaches out from them to the world.

Never before has man been potentially so near to man as now. Within the past half-century, we have seen distances that kept people weeks and months apart reduced to days and hours. We have ceased to wonder that at the twist of a button in our living room we can bring there the form and voice of a person thousands of miles away. Men have dreamed for centuries of reaching the stars; today modern invention has brought that achievement within the realm of possibility.

But how near have men really come to one another? How close are nations? What is nearness? One may sit beside another whose thoughts are continents away and be as distant from him as his wandering thoughts. There is a distance that is not of space, and a nearness that miles cannot invade.

How much of this nearness have men achieved in these fifty years marked by the division of two tragic world wars and many smaller conflicts?

Strangely enough, despite the breaking up of old concepts of stability and the shifting of borders, a certain nearness of man to man is emerging as men unite within the realm of humanitarian concepts.

People join together to help other people, not because they are of the same family, the same community, or even the same country, but just because they are human beings in distress. Such drawing together of men stems from a spiritual impetus whether or not they recognize it—love in its broadest sense.

At the time of the laying of the cornerstone of the United Nations building in New York—significantly, a glass house—Gen. Carlos P. Romulo, of the Philippines, then President of the UN General Assembly, quoted the words of Abraham Lincoln to a nation rent by civil war in 1861: "We are not enemies, but friends. We must not be enemies. Though passion may have strained, it must not break our bonds of affection. The mystic chords of memory, stretching from every battlefield, and patriot grave, to every living heart and hearthstone, all over this broad land, will yet swell the chorus of Union, when again touched, as surely they will be, by the better angels of our nature."

Recalling these words again in an address in Maryland in 1958, General Romulo said he remembered them with "a sense of historic continuity, for their burden has been borne aloft and carried over to the present. The Charter of the United Nations, a copy of which has been encased in the cornerstone, is a call to the nations to be friends not enemies. It is a testament to the brotherhood of man and the indissoluble solidarity of the human family."

He also pointed out that on issues involving human liberty or the fundamental rights of man, the UN "close ranks of their own accord, bound by a unity of purpose which no ironclad alliance can surpass or improve upon."

When the family unit was strong and bound its members to one another by custom and tradition for protection, mutual help, and support, this unit also marked the boundary where the responsibility ended.

But throughout the world, great changes have come which have disrupted the old pattern of family life. In Japan, for instance, the family unit used to include all near relatives. If a woman were widowed, she returned to the family home. If someone were unfortunate or in need, he could look to the family to care for him. Now, the family unit consists legally only of parents and children, and more social legislation is being asked for to provide for those who formerly quite naturally would have looked to relatives for care in time of need. Citizens must join hands now on a broader basis to help one another.

In parts of Asia and Europe, where vast numbers of people have been displaced and families separated, through no fault of their own, millions have become dependent on the aid of others outside the family circle for survival in the past two decades.

The family unit, although still cherished, no longer stands for stability by itself. Relief and rehabilitation—inadequate as they may have seemed before humanity's overwhelming need—have been impelled by concepts of justice, freedom, and compassion. Within these concepts men have joined together to aid one another. The unit of concern is the human family and the cohesive force, love and compassion for mankind.

Men and women the world over who are touched by the needs and aspirations of other men, impelled by this motive to help the human family, find themselves in positions where this deep purpose can gain expression. Dr. Galo Plaza Lasso, President of Ecuador from 1948 to 1952, former Ambassador to the United States, and later chairman of the UN Observer Group in Lebanon, first expressed his concern for the welfare of others by social work among the families on his own hacienda.

Inspired by his example, his daughter, Luz Avelina Plaza, with the same desire to improve the lot of people, pursued a practical education in her own country, the United States, and Europe, and is serving now as a home demonstration agent in Quito.

In Iran there are 4-D Clubs patterned after the 4-H Clubs for girls and boys in the United States. Mrs. Ezzat Aghevli, national supervisor of the home economics extension program of the Iranian Government, with twenty young women working under her, living in the villages, is helping to lift the standards for rural families in Iran by methods similar to those used to improve rural living in the United States. Thus, lessons learned by families in one part of the world provide a pattern to help families in other lands through man's growing interest in the welfare of mankind.

Many of the old props have slipped from under modern society, and it has been forced to find new values and new foundations on which to stand. These may be less material, but they are often more substantial than some of the artificial standards of the past.

In many regions, both parents in a family are engaged in business or industry. They merge their fields of interest with a new sense of partnership in which each may share a larger appreciation of the other's responsibilities. Aware of their community and its influence on the home and likewise aware of the influence of home on community, they reach out from theirs with a contribution of ideas and energy for the improvement of the area in which they live. Here they join with likeminded neighbors to help one another and to help themselves. They are united by common goals.

In the United States, youth centers, libraries, playgrounds, and numerous other civic improvements are the result of such cooperation.

But within a family, community, nation, or family of nations, there also may be conflicting aims and ambitions which are divisive. The walls of a home, confines of a community, or boundaries of a nation cannot hold people together. But there are enduring ties—those that spring from a common interest in the welfare of the human race—of human beings. Such ties are forged by love, compassion, and charity which begin in the heart, therefore in the home, and reach out from there.

5.

This reaching out is not stopped by geography or politics. It occurs in the Communist world as well as in the free.

Sir Winston Churchill, in one of his great postwar addresses, made the following statement:

"Laws just or unjust may govern men's actions. Tyrannies may restrain or regulate their words. The machinery of propaganda may pack their minds with falsehood and deny them truth for many generations of time. But the soul of man thus held in trance or frozen in a long night can be awakened by a spark coming from God knows where and in a moment the whole structure of lies and oppression is on trial for its life. Peoples in bondage need never despair."

Those are words of deep and lasting import. They are also the lesson of history, the promise of today and a beacon of hope for the future. They were spoken on March 31, 1949, at the very depth of Stalinism, when the Communist world was held in such a reign of terror, brutality, and enslavement that many an observer wondered if any spark of freedom still dwelt in the heart and thought of Eastern Europe.

Yet within little more than four years of their utterance the populace of Communist-controlled East Berlin had risen to demand and to obtain concessions from their Moscow-directed overlords. And within seven-and-a-half years Poland had actually won a measure of independence from Soviet control, while Hungary had, for a few days at least, won total independence and stood free of the enslavement in which the Red Army held it.

True, in 1958 as this is written, there has been regression since those days of 1953 and 1956. East Berlin is still firmly in Communist hands; Poland has felt obliged to curtail somewhat its portion of independence, while suffering Hungary has seen the reimposition of Soviet imperialism and brutal repression.

Nevertheless, the message is clear and unmistakable. Peoples in bondage do not, indeed, as Sir Winston said, need ever despair. The knowledge of mankind's right to freedom and justice, the elevation of men's ideals and aspiration, and the ferment which today is taking place in the thinking of all humanity guarantee the eventual triumph of justice and the disappearance of tyranny.

The events in East Berlin, Hungary, Poland, and elsewhere are confirmation that no amount of suppression, whether mental or physical, can quench that spark of which Sir Winston spoke and which will in the end put tyranny on trial for its life.

It has long been obvious that there is a real and growing ferment within the thinking of the Communist world and that this applies as much to the Soviet Union itself as to its satellites. Just what this ferment will mean, we do not yet fully know. But the evidence indicates that in the long run, it will result in greater freedom and democracy.

This can be said, even though this ferment is not in every case necessarily taking the peoples involved in exactly the direction which Western democracy might advocate. It can be said, even though this mental stir carries with it no automatic guarantee of big changes in Communistdom in the immediate future.

For it shows that, despite all attempts at mental regimentation, men insist upon exercising the power of independent thought, that today no barriers of censorship are wholly successful, and that the desire for truth is a universal longing.

Confining oneself to the Soviet Union, the stir taking place there could not be described by a Western observer as either treasonous or revolutionary, however severely the Kremlin might be inclined to view it.

Rather, it could be described as a critical questing, as a search for a more satisfying ideal combined with a growing dissatisfaction with many of the more repressive and stultifying aspects of Communist life.

While only a tiny portion of the population may be able to define to itself the exact form which its dissatisfaction takes, a much larger portion is known to experience this dissatisfaction to varying degrees.

Paradoxically, this ferment has grown with the development of certain advantages and privileges within the Communist world. As that world continues to expand its educational and productive faculties, there is created an ever-greater number of individuals, who, while considering themselves faithful Marxists and loyal Soviet citizens, are nonetheless inclined to be increasingly critical of certain aspects of Soviet life.

Foremost among these are the intellectual classes, whose

contacts with Western literature and thinking, even though drastically limited, have created an obvious dissatisfaction with the Communist policy of rigidly regulating all aspects of intellectual life.

These are followed by the "successful" members of Soviet society—the managerial, professional, and professorial classes, the men and women whose value to their country has brought them special rewards.

Although satisfied with these rewards and in many cases grateful to the system which conferred them, these individuals show a strong desire to rid their country of those arbitrary and repressive powers which can, in a moment, strip them of all their advantages.

Although it is too early to say that these feelings on the part of either the intellectual or the professional classes constitute a serious threat to the Soviet system, there is evidence that their attitude has resulted in a number of steps which have modified the all-out terror and repression which characterized life in the Soviet Union prior to the passing of Stalin in March, 1953.

The ferment of thought within intellectual circles has been demonstrated in many ways. The earliest evidence came with the so-called "thaw" which set in shortly after Stalin's demise. In the first three to four years there were produced in the Soviet Union a number of works of literature which would have been unthinkable prior to that time.

There was also a somewhat greater freedom of discussion which, according to all evidence, the citizens found highly stimulating. Similarly, the average individual showed delight at the intellectual and artistic contacts with the West which resulted from this "thaw."

It was this period which saw the emergence of several literary works which bespoke the questioning and agitation

which lie beneath the well-plastered surface of Soviet life.
Best known of these works are the novels *Not by Bread Alone*
and *Doctor Zhivago,* each of which was categoric proof that
four decades of thought control had not succeeded in destroying independent thought within the Communist world.

By the Communists' own admission, the events in Hungary
and Poland in the fall of 1956 were sparked and partially
directed by the dissatisfied intellectuals of those two countries. In a like manner, it was among the intellectuals of the
Soviet Union that the greatest doubt was expressed regarding the justification for Soviet intervention in Hungary.

Indeed, so deep did this doubt go, that there are well-
authenticated cases of Soviet university students openly ex-
pressing disbelief when their professors proffered the officially
obligatory explanation of the Red Army's suppression of
Hungarian freedom.

It may be useful to quote from an article which appeared
in *The Christian Science Monitor* in 1958 which detailed the
views of a Soviet graduate student, now in the West, on why
summit conferences open new windows in the thinking of
the average citizen of a Communist country.

"With respect to at least two points, the Geneva Conference [of 1955] was seen to have been a defeat for the
Soviet leaders. 'In the initial acceptance of the Eden Plan
for holding free elections for all of Germany [the Soviet
intelligentsia] saw the tacit recognition of the fact that
elections in East Germany were not free....'

"Rejection of Mr. Dulles' proposals [for the broadening
of cultural exchanges] was generally interpreted as an expression of apprehension that the solidity of the Soviet
ideological position might suffer from a continuous debate
with the West."

For many years it was a characteristic of the Communist

movement that its followers believed that "the end justified the means." In that spirit they were prepared to put up with and excuse the most flagrant violations of elementary human dignity, decency, and kindness. Large numbers of Communists still hold to this barbaric standard, but there is proof that the percentage so doing is dwindling.

Following the revelations of Stalin's brutality, in the wake of the Hungarian tragedy, and as a result of the recent execution of four Hungarian patriots, there has been a deep stir among Communist followers in the West and a number of resignations from the various parties.

While it would be wishful thinking to believe that this had dealt a fatal blow to communism, we are nevertheless justified in seeing in it a further indication of the growing tendency to question both the methods and the ideology of communism.

When such questioning and evolution will finally destroy or remake Communist tyranny no one can say. Without some international cataclysm, the process may be slow and gradual, requiring perhaps decades and almost certainly years. But it is impossible to view the Communist scene and not to see that a deep ferment is at work and that, as time goes by, it will feed increasingly upon itself.

6.

We have seen that, behind the Iron Curtain, the survival of independent thought has shown itself in the work of the writers Boris Pasternak (*Doctor Zhivago*) and Vladimir Dudintsev (*Not by Bread Alone*). In the free world independent thought has not only survived but flourished in the literature leading to the future. Spiritual values, however, have been less obvious, perhaps because serious twentieth-century literature has been occupied more with testing values than with affirming them, and even some writers of spiritual intent have obscured their purposes for the general reader through difficulties of style or harshness of language and subject matter.

At the end of the nineteenth century William Dean Howells was questioning the freedom to write novels unfit for the eyes of young ladies. In the middle of the twentieth century young ladies were writing novels that might have shocked Howells himself.

This kind of change just about sums up the literary situation for many of today's general readers. They think that all the old bars are down. And they are repelled—or attracted— by the thought.

But sales and translation figures suggest that these general readers have been reading little of the twentieth-century writing that the literary world has considered of prime significance. This may not always have been to the discredit of the general readers. But it means that they may have missed the broad trend of experiment and reappraisal in which the new freedom—or sometimes license—has been only a part.

The world's serious literature has been passing through a half century of exciting, deplorable, rewarding, ridiculous exploration. It has tested the limits of language, form, behavior, psychology, values. It has looked down into the recesses of human personality and out into the political and social spheres where communism, fascism, and democracy do battle.

It probably has broken down as much as it has built up. But there are signs that it is entering a new phase—a time of consolidation, perhaps, when gains can be identified and accepted, losses recognized and written off.

In 1922 came two works that helped to make the period between the world wars the one that seems most characteristic of twentieth-century literary experiment, though the ferment had begun earlier on the Continent. T. S. Eliot's poem, *The Waste Land,* presented a philosophically bleak but poetically rich picture of a sterile society. Through such elements as fragmented form, recondite allusions explained in pages of notes (which Eliot has recently asserted were written, or at least expanded, to lengthen a rather slim volume!), Eliot made something new of his borrowings from the Elizabethans and the French symbolists, something that has affected almost all subsequent poetry.

James Joyce's novel *Ulysses,* offered an intricate parallel to Homer's *Odyssey* in an Irish setting. It not only drew attention on grounds of obscenity but displayed a virtuoso command of language, myth, and symbol, and indicated the potentialities of the stream of consciousness technique for revealing character.

This was the year in which the best-selling novels in the United States were *If Winter Comes, The Sheik,* and Booth Tarkington's *Gentle Julia.*

To take another sample, 1926 also brought two works that are still being studied—something that cannot exactly be said for the year's best-selling fiction—*The Private Life of Helen of Troy* and *Gentlemen Prefer Blondes.*

It was the year of the first German edition of Franz Kafka's *The Castle,* an expressionistic narrative about an ambiguous character named K. and his ambiguous progress toward an ambiguous goal. Sometimes compared to, sometimes hotly dissociated from, *Pilgrim's Progress,* it still gives theologians, philosophers, psychoanalysts, and sociologists material for argument.

Also in 1926 appeared Ernest Hemingway's *The Sun Also Rises,* in which the American author—significantly an expatriate—focused the rootlessness and despair of a generation while displaying a stripped but evocative prose style that probably has been the major single influence on the American prose that followed.

Unlike a Dickens, who courted the public and became a classic anyway, many twentieth-century innovators made few concessions to readers who had not caught up with their psychological, sociological, anthropological, or semantic enthusiasms. Yet their influence has been seen not only in later serious literature but in popular entertainment—the "hard-boiled" detective story with echoes of Hemingway's prose, the movie dream sequence recalling the surrealists, the introspective television play with a debt to the psychological novelists.

But none of the writers just named is represented among the first one hundred best sellers of the century in America, even including paperback sales, as listed in *Sixty Years of Best Sellers: 1895-1955*. Nor, on the international level, is any of them among the first fifty of the "most translated" authors determined by UNESCO for 1948-55 (though Hemingway is high in the second fifty).

The same holds true for other influential authors such as William Faulkner, William Butler Yeats, Thomas Mann, Luigi Pirandello, D. H. Lawrence, Marcel Proust, Joseph Conrad, and probably the most famous (though not for his novels) literary personality of the century, George Bernard Shaw.

Some of the between-wars writers kept on writing after World War II, but few of their later works have equaled their best early ones in critical acclaim. And of the novelists who have emerged since the war few have reached similar stature in the critics' estimation.

The 1957 winner of the Nobel Prize for literature, Albert Camus of France, is one likely candidate for continuing international attention. He seems to reflect a kind of yearning for religion among intellectuals who are not content with obeisance to the old orthodoxies. He is less notable for his manner than for his substance, his pessimistic, but not hopeless, probing of human motives and morality.

In the United States, J. D. Salinger, a leader in what has come to be called the *New Yorker* (magazine) school of fiction, likewise shows a concern for religion in the broad sense in stories that speak to, and perhaps for, an intellectual segment of the postwar college generation.

In Britain, the various "angry young men" are lumped together to their dismay. Paced by the satire of Kingsley Amis and the wrathy plays of John Osborne, they lash out, in the best style of rebellious youth, at a society they did not create. But they are not always simply negative, and among the fire and the fumes are gleams of longing for honest emotion, individuality, and—here, too—religion in a time of too much comfortable materialism under the shadow of the bomb.

Along with the new gropings for values, however, there have been few gropings for new forms. Today's young poets, university trained and often university supported, are more likely to turn to classical models than to the extremes of their immediate forebears. The youngest novelists, at least in America, seem intent on straightforward realism, leaving allegory and symbolism to the past.

Today's most notorious "experimental" writing probably belongs to America's "beat generation" authors, who use ill-digested literary allusions and the slang of "hipster" jazz fans, among other things, to rhapsodize on a wild neoromantic world of sex, narcotics, wanderlust, and the search for "ecstasy."

Does the lessening of experiment mean the literary future

will be dull? Not necessarily. No one would want to undo the
recent era of questing for new things to say and new ways to
say them—or want to prevent another one in the years ahead.
But in the interim perhaps writers can profitably concentrate
on such time-honored qualities of style as simplicity, lucidity,
vitality, and such time-honored qualities of content as a
balanced view of the human condition.

At least three works come to mind, not as landmarks perhaps but as hints of the possibilities.

C. P. Snow, the atomic age's major novelist who is also
a physicist, has completed seven volumes in a series of novels,
Strangers and Brothers, which is proving that a complex
modern society (in this case in Britain) can be treated
fictionally in a temperate, traditional, yet absorbing way.

In *Cry, the Beloved Country,* Alan Paton of South Africa
showed how the long-range problem of humanity, race relations, can be illuminated in a novel of compassion, moral
sense, and thoroughly accessible prose.

In a recent Pulitzer Prize novel, *A Death in the Family,* the
late James Agee of the United States dealt with an individual
but basic human situation in a truly observed story of the
family of a child whose father is killed. From his experience
as a screen writer and film critic, Agee might have been expected to experiment with cinematic devices in his novel,
as writers had done before him. Instead, so far as one can
judge from an unfinished work, he went further—to the poetic
point where technique has been fully assimilated—and re-
tained the pictorial precision of the camera without its obvious tricks.

This may be one direction of the serious literature of tomorrow, toward a warm but unblinking regard for humanity
expressed through traditional craftsmanship that draws selectively on the weird and wonderful experiments of yesterday.

In that event, it almost sounds as if the public, as well as the literati, might be interested.

Certainly the public of the future will have little economic excuse for not reading books. In addition to the expanding facilities of the free public library, the phenomenon of paperback publishing in the twentieth century has made many of the world's classics as conveniently available as toothpaste—and for about the same price.

When tomorrow's pundits are adding up the technological advances of today, they may decide that the temperamental "hardware" for space satellites was no more significant than the faithful rubberplate presses that began turning out twelve thousand books an hour.

At least the potential for far-reaching significance lies in those presses. If they lead the mass audience to the best of books—instead of the worst, which are also represented in their output—the effect could be more powerful than the bomb.

"That guy Homer certainly can write. Send me another by him," said the reader of a paperback *Odyssey*, according to a story that has been making the literary rounds in various versions. For the reader to whom bookstores and libraries are forbidding strongholds of scholarship, the drugstore-news-stand-vending-machine paperback may be the welcome sign to new riches of thought and feeling. With literacy increasing all over the globe, the paperback exploration of the inner universe seems a natural accompaniment to rocket trips to the moon.

The sex-and-violence thrillers, with their lurid covers, have not disappeared from the stands. Sometimes even unobjectionable books are bedizened in a way to alienate the very readers who might appreciate them most.

But the peak of pictorial vulgarity seems to have passed.

Every once in a while a more-or-less penitential voice from the industry admits to a time of competitive excesses and says that more taste and restraint are now being used. A glance at the display racks tends to confirm this claim.

One reason is the increasing proportion of "quality" paperbacks. While these are not always carried at the usual paperback distribution points, their sales have been rising at a faster rate than that of the staple mysteries, westerns, and other routine paperback fare.

At the same time there has been an increase in paperback "originals" as distinguished from the reprints of hardbound books that always have formed the bulk of paperback publication. While many of the originals are cheap fiction ground out to time-worn specification, others are books of the highest seriousness.

In some cases, reversing the usual process, they find a place in hard covers after first being published in paper. In this way, paperbacks can provide the publisher with a trial balloon for little-known authors whose merit seems more certain than their immediate commerical potentiality.

Books for how-to-do-it, self-improvement, and reference purposes have been among the leaders in paperback sales. In the United States, for example, the best-selling paperback, surpassing even the mush and mayhem of Mickey Spillane, is probably Benjamin Spock's *Pocket Book of Baby and Child Care.*

Schools and colleges are adopting paperbacks for texts. University presses have begun to publish them. The whole development could hardly have been imagined by the present-day publishers who started this "benign revolution," as it has been called—or by scholarly Aldus Manutius of Venice, who started printing a pocket series of classics in 1501 (and in the process invented italic type).

In the nineteenth century the paperback book had flourishing periods in both Europe and America. For example, the Tauchnitz Editions of Leipzig brought more than five thousand English and American titles, in the original language, to the Continent. Beginning at about the same time, the Boston Society for the Diffusion of Knowledge sponsored inexpensive paper editions in the United States.

American paperbacks became more prominent in the latter part of the century when the proportion of paperback titles to hardbound far exceeded that of today. A notable European venture was Reclam's Universal Bibliothek in Germany, with its thousands of classics sold in millions of copies at the equivalent of ten cents apiece.

In England "chapbooks"—cheap books—arrived soon after the coming of printing itself. But it was not until 1935, with the beginning of Penguin Books, that paperbacks, as they are known there today, really leaped ahead.

Meanwhile, the Albatross Modern Continental Library had started in Hamburg and eventually took over Tauchnitz. Shortly thereafter, in 1939, Pocket Books began publishing in the United States. In 1948 the American branch of Penguin became the independent New American Library of World Literature.

Now many other companies—and countries—have entered the field. Supplementing local publishing, English-language paperbacks go around the world to Asia, Africa, and the Middle East. In the United States and Canada, which have the fewest regular bookstores per capita of sixteen countries studied by UNESCO, there are a hundred thousand or about ten times as many, outlets for paperback books.

The Soviet Union remains conspicuous as a country of high literacy with no paperback industry. On the other hand, the

Soviet Union provides ordinary hardbound books at a comparatively low price.

Allowing for the dirt and the triviality, paperbacks are, for both the publisher and the reader, the book bonanza of the age. They have reached the point where the American Association for the Advancement of Science can offer a lengthy check list of books for the Paperbound Science Library; Boston's education television station, WGBH-TV, can put together a series of programs on paperbacks; a thirty-page index can be prepared listing nineteen hundred paperbacks for college classroom use.

"Scholarship which is never made conveniently available to those who want it is ineffectual," said the University of Chicago Press in announcing its intention to board the paperback band wagon.

Well, scholarship, science, poetry, art, biography, drama, history, how-to-do-it, fiction—it *has* been made conveniently available. Both paperbacks and their readership promise to grow in the future.

7.

Meanwhile, the arts other than literature are also expected to continue their progress toward appreciation by a wider and wider public. Questions are raised about the depth of this appreciation. But the fact remains that, whether he takes advantage of it or not, the average individual has more opportunity than ever before to become acquainted with the insights of the artist.

While changes have been taking place in the long established fields of the arts during the past fifty years, fresh enterprises, no less significant, have been finding new and larger audiences to understand and enjoy them.

One of the most conspicuous of the new developments is

the steadily increasing number of festivals. There are music festivals, dance festivals, theater festivals, and movie festivals. They begin early in the spring and they may be found until autumn.

There are now three Stratfords paying honor to Shakespeare—the original one in England, another in Ontario, and a third in Connecticut. Music festivals run the gamut from jazz to symphonies—or perhaps the order should be reversed. Once upon a time, summer was a quiet period in the arts. Now plays and operas follow audiences out of the city and bring them in throngs to performances in the mountains, at the seashore, and in the country.

At the same time, the mass media are bringing the arts into the home. Hi-fi and now the new stereophonic recordings make available the classics and the newest of the music played by world-renowned orchestras or presented by noted soloists. Operas may be heard and studied in the quiet of the living room.

Musicals from the current stage may be enjoyed at home on recordings by people who never will be able to see a Broadway performance. Thousands who never will hear My Fair Lady in a theater have listened to its music from a turntable. Enduring plays from the great store of dramatic literature have been inscribed on disks by stars of the first magnitude.

In even larger degree, television makes its contribution, with its steady diet of films and occasional offerings of greater artistic stature. Radio continues to play its part.

Entertainment, which once was to be found away from home, now pursues its audience to the fireside. Instead of being sought, entertainment now is to be chosen; the problem has become one of selection.

These latter-day diversions—the movies, television, hi-fi

record players—have offered the live theater stiff competition.

In 1908, there were 2,900 legitimate playhouses in the United States; by 1953, according to a Yale University survey, there were 234. Thirty years ago it was common for more than 250 plays to open in New York each season. Broadway openings during 1957-58 totaled 77, according to the *New York Times*, with only 71 in 1958-59.

With motion pictures in a shaken condition and TV reaching perhaps the lowest level of quality in its short history, playgoing may win back young people in the late teens and early twenties who have traditionally been counted among the theater's partisans. Such a positive development will owe much to the burgeoning off-Broadway movement.

The 1957-58 season was one of off-Broadway's busiest. According to *Variety:* "An estimated $600,000 was invested in off-Broadway production. . . . That amount, equal to the cost of two full-scale Broadway musicals, represented the total outlay for 59 Equity-bonded presentations, exclusive of the Phoenix Theater offerings." The Phoenix, a large playhouse which operates on a different basis from other off-Broadway theaters, has for five seasons been providing unusual theater fare.

Twenty-nine off-Broadway productions were new plays, in itself perhaps the most conspicuous sign of the growing significance of the activity that goes on in converted lofts, transformed walk-through apartments, basements, halls, and a few actual playhouses. The remainder of the repertory was provided by contemporary Europeans, standard works, and classics by O'Casey, Shaw, and Shakespeare.

In general it can be said:

That the American theater's greatest accomplishment of the half century has been its survival.

That the playgoer of the twenties and early thirties witnessed a period of artistic achievement and theatrical brilliance which has never been surpassed in the United States.

That the principal characteristic of the American stage in 1958 was a consistently high level of competence which sometimes rose to the pinnacles of theater art.

That an accent on the broodingly personal and sometimes neurotic has not meant the exclusion of the drama's sunnier moods or of its concern with mankind's loftier motives.

That the very commercialism which lamentably dogs the theater possesses at least the positive virtue of demanding the best efforts of which artists and artisans are capable.

At the same time, in Great Britain, though hundreds of theaters have closed down in the last half century, the dramatic picture for the future, relatively, is not dark. The competition of the cinema reached its peak in the early 1930's, and has since declined. It is the cinema rather than the theater that the spread of television alarms most.

In one respect the taste of the public has considerably improved. Shakespeare has not only ceased to empty the theaters where he is played. He now is the most popular playwright in the world. He draws larger audiences than Jean Anouilh, Tennessee Williams, or Terence Rattigan. There are nearly twenty important productions of his plays in England every year—that is, one every three weeks, besides innumerable amateur presentations. At Stratford and the Old Vic, devoted entirely to Shakespeare, there is scarcely ever a vacant seat.

This is due at least partly to the fact that Britain's leading players—John Gielgud, Sir Laurence Olivier, Michael Redgrave, Donald Wolfit, Ralph Richardson—like to play Shakespeare; so they reinforce the dramatist with their own great personal popularity. Nor do they confine themselves to the obvious choices, such as *Hamlet* and *Lear*.

Olivier has shown that a magnificent tragedy, a tragedy of a great man pushed to the last extremes of weariness, yet still retaining traces of his younger grandeur, is to be found in *Titus Andronicus,* a piece hitherto thought to be a mere barbarity. Richardson made out of the last quarter of an hour of *Timon of Athens* a thing of unexpected and indeed radiant beauty. Paul Scofield at Stratford toward the end of the forties began a new assessment of *Troilus and Cressida,* once despised, which now ranks it among Shakespeare's very greatest plays.

But, though Shakespeare is a good foundation for the British theater, he cannot be its sole strength. Its continuing vitality must rest on the production of new plays. There now is a strong demand from the younger people interested in the theater that it should be not merely a form of entertainment, but a vital contribution to the social scene.

This feeling is generally expressed in the assertion that the drama should be "committed" to the solution of social problems.

Plays, however—and perhaps it is just as well—are not written by "climates of opinion," but by playwrights. And the new playwrights who now are figuring upon the English scene—John Osborne, Paul Shaffer, author of *Five Finger Exercise,* John Mortimer, Robert Bolt, and some others—are committed, if they are committed at all, not to any particular theory but to their own individual view of life. So far as one can see into the future, they have the vitality to keep the British theater flourishing, and flourishing in the individualistic way which in the past has been its glory.

In France, the picture is less clear. It was by the "committed" drama of Jean-Paul Sartre and Albert Camus that the French theater gained the lead in the postwar theater. At the moment the "committed" drama is hesitant; the most popular plays in France are now boulevard comedies, while the intellectual leadership of the theater has passed into the hands of Eugene Ionesco and Samuel Beckett, who are concerned with their own private worlds much more than with the problems of politics.

All the arts continue to face the problem of balancing private and generally recognizable worlds in illuminating man's relation to man. In the best of the emerging music and painting, for example, the effect contributes to freedom for spiritual unfoldment, though at times almost the opposite has seemed to be the case.

For the listener brought up on traditional music, the efforts of Schönberg, Stravinsky, and their followers may be puzzling to say the least. What are the "contemporary" composers up to?

Schönberg began working in the post-Wagnerian school of chromatic harmony; and while still a young man he felt that our tonal harmonic system, that which had prevailed for centuries and which still prevails, had said all that it could be made to say. So he decided to leave the realms of tonality and to explore the realms of atonality—or a system of music which broke completely with the established system of harmony.

He devised what he called "a technique for composing with 12 tones," a technique too complicated to explain briefly. But his system has since attracted hundreds of young composers into his ranks. Some have used his technique in its strictest terms; others have modified it in their own various ways. Schönberg's explorations have thus resulted in the most difficult kind of music for uninitiated listeners to understand.

Stravinsky, while still a young man, created *Le Sacre du Printemps,* a work that will remain the most important musical milestone in the first half of the twentieth century; for, with its fearless methods of combining melodies, as well as its extraordinary polyrhythmic structure (superimposing various rhythms one upon another), Stravinsky gave the signal to other composers that anything was possible. He at once became a leader who has since attracted more followers than has Schönberg.

Here are several points to bear in mind while seeking an understanding of contemporary music:

1. The amount of dissonance is not what determines the worth or worthlessness of a piece of music. Dissonance has always been an integral part of our harmonic system; it is plentiful, for example, in the works of Bach, Beethoven, and Wagner.

True, it is more abundant in contemporary music. Our ears have become educated to accept the amount of dissonance used by older composers; we must give our ears time and exercise to feel at home with the dissonance of today.

Remember, too, that dissonance is not necessarily discord. A discord may be thought of as a mistake, as when a child plays notes that have not been set down by the composer. Dissonance is the intentional use of conflicting tones for an emotional or dramatic effect.

The value of a piece of music is not to be determined by its school, its idiom, or its dissonance content. It is determined by the quality of its inspiration. The inspired composer will eventually be heard, regardless of the system he employs.

2. We will find the road easier if we do not expect contemporary music to sound like the music we already know and appreciate. Music has been defined as "ordered sound," and sound may be ordered in many different ways. Oriental music is no less music because it is not ordered according to Western systems. In like manner, modern music is no less music because it is not ordered according to older traditions.

3. Music is an emotional language. We cannot expect to respond to the poetry of a new musical language without first learning the language, any more than we can respond to poems written in Polish or Hungarian without first learning those languages.

4. Willingness to listen several times to a difficult piece is very helpful. Repetition educates the ear to heretofore unaccustomed combinations of tones.

5. The desire to understand and the patience to keep listening—these qualities of thought will always make the way easier until the door swings wide on the new musical world.

In painting, too, vanguard artists of the earlier years of this century turned their backs upon their teachers, upon precept and precedent. Undaunted, they cut new paths in the direction of free, nontraditional, personal expression.

Rebellion was in the air. The impressionists had announced their independence of schools. They went outdoors to paint; they divided color. Their disciples altered, exaggerated, distorted imagery. A younger generation broke up form, dismantled, disjointed elements of design that had hitherto seemed absolutes. The trend toward breaking up physical properties and destroying theoretical methods has been carried to the ultimate by artists of our time.

Dynamics is the keynote. The artist is suggesting in an emblematic way the overwhelming advances of natural science. There is also a counterpart of psychological exploration. Many a contemporary artist is concerned with the psychic states of modern man, with finding a line, color, and form syntax that will suggest urges and perturbations of today.

New devices for cogent expression have been invented; for example, the movable focus and the double image, or the visual pun. Often the artist fancies he must disembody rather than shape solidly, destroy rather than build.

As he molds new symbols, pertinent to the modern way of seeing and thinking, the artist seeks fresh sources of imaginative stimulation, in the archaic, primitive, and savage arts. He jettisons the entire baggage of traditional techniques as he emulates the spontaneity of the art of the young child.

Curious contrasts exist in the art world. The more complex the technological world becomes, the more intricate the social problems, the more distracting the successive pressures of international strife, the more eager are some artists to withdraw into an ivory tower, to elude the manifold sensations of average experience, to probe, to search for what to them seems the fundamental meaning of things.

A profusion of optical experiences crowds upon the artist; vast aerial perspectives, natural phenomena discovered through high-powered telescopes and microscopes. The availability of arts of the past in well-stocked art museums, in photography and motion pictures, has virtually numbed his sensibilities. This teeming abundance is not necessarily an advantage. The artist turns his back on observed fact as he strives to visualize unseen forces.

Early in the century there were the Fauves in France, and that rebellious group in Germany known as the Bridge. They pressed toward a maximum of personal expression. The artists who performed as laws unto themselves could be called the modern romantics.

In contrast, the pondered, geometric pursuits of the cubists may be regarded as modern classicism. Cubism gradually became transformed into abstraction. Every trend has been carried to the utmost extreme. Some painters ultimately resolved a picture into the nonhuman idiom of squares, rectangles, and circles.

It can be said that art in the twentieth century has shuttled between the extremes of pure geometry and intimately personal expression. These are the affirmative trends.

There are negative trends also. The surrealistic phase reflects a dismal pessimism, a disillusion concerning world affairs, and savage manifestations of inhumanity. This style exemplifying resignation is only a by-product, for art by definition is a positive pursuit, affirming, not denying, maximum human experience.

Contemporary art may seem meaningless or irrational. In the pursuit of extremes, in the exchange of the beautiful for the ugly, in the preference of chaos for order there may appear to be a complete reversal or discarding of universal values. The modern artist maintains that his objective is not something pleasing, that his deepest desire is to express himself in a fundamental, a profoundly meaningful way.

At this moment it is evident that artists are struggling to restore a balance. Many leading talents are striving to find the lost horizon, to re-establish a social motivation within traceable frontiers, to reinvest the image with human attributes.

The technical rebellion of the twentieth century may seem to have provoked unnecessary chaos and even misadventure in the arts. But the truly responsible artist has gained much from the complete dismantling of textbook disciplines and academic clichés. The procedures of cubism and abstraction have broadened and deepened possibilities, providing the artist with a more flexible language of pictorial communication.

It would be unintelligent to generalize that art will return to a middle way with the re-establishment of a humanistic objective. Art will not be completely stabilized. It never has been. Permanent stabilization is not in the character of the artistic adventure.

The artist will continue to react with extreme sensitiveness to successive accomplishments in technical progress, moral crisis, as well as spiritual growth. If he seems to withdraw from the social scene, to ignore mankind, that is only temporary, for eventually, inevitably, human values and the human drama will exercise a gravitational pull that will bring him back to the fold.

8.

And so we move from the home, the school, the church, through literature and the arts, to the great world and man's relation to man in it. How easy it is to look out upon the face of the earth and teeming humanity with its poverty and slavery to restrictive social modes and be saddened. Or to recall the horrors of Hiroshima and Buchenwald and ask if mankind is far removed from the jungle of barbarism after all the years of human history.

And yet cannot we say with Jesus after he had looked to a future of cataclysms and perfidy, "And when these things begin to pass, then look up, and lift up your heads; for your redemption draweth nigh." There is reason for good cheer and courage as we turn away from such dark images as play across our thoughts of mankind and ask: Has progress been made in man's relationship to man? Has moral sensitivity deepened?

What a remarkable thing it is that a global outcry resounds when a report of racial discrimination spins out of the West. Mankind's moral sensitivity has indeed been sharpened and heightened in the past fifty years to an unparalleled degree.

And Western society has shown that men can be free to live lives of individual joy and accomplishment that leave behind the savage struggle for a crust of bread each day. The world has watched and wants this. Behind this accomplishment is the West's conscientious proclamation of the equality of men. In fact, in the United States Little Rock's ordeal is the aftermath of a cruel war that was fought because of a nation's moral sensitivity to this need. Mankind is asking with outstretched arms for this freedom from discrimination and freedom from want realized in the West.

What is the state of moral sensitivity in the world today which at base will determine whether or not men everywhere will be able to achieve their desires? It can be said without doubt that there is more concern for the welfare of the mass of individuals than ever in history. More fairness, kindness, generosity, and tolerance are being expressed; there are heightened demands for social justice.

The danger is that these demands would sacrifice everything for material ease in a police state, or for a state bureaucracy that crushes initiative and individual hope. It has been said that mankind may settle for the ant heap when it could have the bee hive. The dilemma is well put by C. S. Lewis when he asks, "Is there any possibility of getting the super welfare state's honey and avoiding the sting?"

There is evidence that this is not possible. In the United States there is concern about the willingness of young people to seek security rather than reward. In Sweden an increasing sadness has been described. In Great Britain many have remarked a lessening of initiative, and queues of young people at the immigration offices, particularly at the time of Suez, indicate a certain disenchantment with the socialist atmosphere.

Be that as it may, in the past fifty years the universal moral ferment has brought an ever-increasing concern for individual citizens and their needs. The status of women has progressed to a point of approximate equality in many nations. Mass education has advanced. Laws are less brutal.

Criminals are viewed with more compassion. The slave trade is limited to a few dark corners of the earth. Racial segregation is waning. The traffic of drugs and narcotics is increasingly policed. And it can be said that the colonial burden has been eased in a way that would not have been possible if the moral idea of equality for all men had not moved out into the global consciousness so powerfully that it could not be denied.

The very existence of the United Nations, and the League of Nations before it, is due to a global conscience, and that moral sensitivity was never more sharply delineated than during the Suez crisis in 1956, when a UN debate sounded over motivations. The UN in recent years has taken a deep interest in such disparate problems as disarmament, the landings in Lebanon and Jordan and the entire vexed Middle East question, the Hungarian repression, the peaceful uses of atomic energy, and the questions of Algeria, Cyprus, Dutch New Guinea, and South Africa. And at the time of the attack on South Korea a historic moral condemnation was voted, and an international force began to come into being.

The UN has expanded its social and economic activities. Economic commissions for Europe, Asia, and Latin America have been active, working along with the financing of progress for poverty-stricken peoples.

Through the UN there has been as well a global effort to lift labor standards through the International Labor Organization which actually began in 1919. Then there are the World Health Organization, the Food and Agricultural Organization, and the Educational, Scientific and Cultural Organization.

It is interesting to listen to Arnold Toynbee who wrote, "My own guess is that our age will be remembered chiefly neither for its horrifying crimes nor its astonishing inventions, but for its having been the first age since the dawn of civilization, some five or six thousand years back, in which people dared to think it practicable to make the benefits of civilization available to the whole human race."

Mankind is moving toward the perfection of the high ideals which underlie the mutual trust which makes any society possible. In the face of industrialization, population pressures, hydrogen bombs, and the mad ambition of dictatorships, this basic moral sensitivity is often obscured and even forgotten. Yet it is there, for man is there.

V

NATIONS LIVING TOGETHER

Potentials for Peace

1.

NATIONS ARE THE SUMS OF MEN. AS MEN GAIN FREEDOM FOR
spiritual unfoldment, nations gain freedom from war. In the
days ahead the threats of war are great, but the potentials
for peace are greater.

Despite the severest tensions, there are examples today
of how nations can live together in the ever more crowded
world of the future. This is worth remembering as we
analyze first the problems and the dangers. Too often civil
decency and law-abiding tendencies are overlooked in the
rush to weigh sputniks against ICBMs and come out with
judgments for the future of mankind based solely on technological progress.

Defense is necessary as a deterrent. But once aggression is
deterred this is not enough. Deterrents such as the Strategic
Air Command and a powerful United States Navy only give
us time. Time for what? Time to build a real peace. Time to
assure brotherhood. Time to feed men's longing for freedom,
justice, education, and lives of dignity.

No society on the face of the earth could exist without the
preponderance of trust and mutual sympathy and understanding between individuals. All this helps to cement so-

ciety. People pay their bills, stop when the light turns red, dive into the water to save a drowning child as a matter of course. When we build for peace and brotherhood in the world, we are building on these normal and natural tendencies of men. In the time that is earned by arming to the teeth, mankind must turn to the further cementing of society.

Meanwhile, the arms race leads to problems and dangers. Both the United States and the Soviet Union have stockpiles of atomic and hydrogen bombs. By commonly accepted estimates, each has enough such warheads to demolish every conceivable military target in the other country, laying waste practically every city and destroying its inhabitants, to contaminate the whole world's atmosphere with deadly radiation for centuries to come, and to have unused bombs left over if the early salvos could be delivered through the opponent's defenses.

Under these circumstances, the two leading world powers, to use a simile employed by an atomic scientist, are like two scorpions in a bottle, either of which could fatally sting the other but would itself be fatally stung in the process. This is the "atomic stalemate."

Mankind has seldom refrained from war because of the terribleness of the weapons involved; but there are kinds of warfare from which nations have drawn back because the consequence, not only to the enemy, but also to neutrals and possibly themselves might be impossible to calculate or might exceed any possible gain. Examples are chemical and bacterial warfare. Sober judgment by heads of nations may put nuclear combat in the same category.

Missile development or some other innovation may alter the balance but at present rates of military progress this stalemate or standoff apparently will exist for several years, if not indefinitely.

Though there is no firm word on Soviet missile capability, there are some informed estimates that the Soviets have had 1,500-mile missiles operational since 1957 and that their 5,000-mile missiles are not far behind.

The United States, by contrast, is not expected to have its 5,000-mile Atlas—which can be fired from the United States— until 1960 or after.

Thus, assuming current estimates are correct, the Soviet now is in a position to shower Europe, Southern Asia, and North Africa with missiles and is, or shortly will be, in a position to strike continental United States.

This, according to military specialists, is not as serious a threat to the free world as it appears on the surface.

The United States has more than enough bombers to obliterate Soviet Union bases several times over with nuclear bombs.

It is probably sufficient to say that, if both countries keep up their present pace of missile development, neither one is likely to get too far ahead for a long period.

There is always danger that an intercontinental war may be started by mistake, but the United States has described the careful double-checking system under which its pilots operate to prevent this from their side.

What confronts the nations may not be an extension of diplomacy into war as a means of reaching national or ideological objectives. It may be instead a searching diplomacy and statecraft to find substitutes for war—at least for general or all-out war—by which to advance national or other interests.

This may not quite mean the "moral equivalent for war" which William James hoped would be found, though it may tend in that direction. Obviously the substitute may be the kind of nibbling operations, "brushfire" wars, and political infiltration at which the Communists on various parts of their periphery from Czechoslovakia to Korea and back to Syria have shown themselves adept. It is also taking the form of competition in trade, credit, and economic assistance.

Americans doubtless would like to choose the economic area for contest, arduous though that may be, and to say with President Eisenhower that "there is no alternative to peace." But they also would agree with what he said at another time, "In the final choice, a soldier's pack is not so heavy as a prisoner's chains."

There is the faint but long-cherished and possibly growing hope that nations ultimately will reach some agreement for limitation and control of nuclear and other armaments. But space—a new dimension for warfare—has added, in like manner, a new and difficult dimension to the problem of controlling weapons of war.

The starting point for control plans is the simple and seemingly logical proposition that space should be used for peaceful purposes only, and that this decision should be enforced.

Such a prohibition, according to students of the problem, would be easier to enforce in the case of orbiting objects than in the case of projectiles. Orbiting objects have a life expectancy of months, if not years or decades; projectiles do their work in minutes—or will, once the count-down period before firing has been reduced.

It would be technically feasible, therefore, disarmament experts say, to control orbiting objects. Would it be politically possible?

The answer to that question depends, in turn, on the question which lies behind all disarmament negotiations: To whose advantage would control be?

It is all very well, diplomats say, for idealists to contend that control would be to everyone's advantage. But governments usually do not base their policies on such a premise unless forced to do so by public opinion. Responsible government leaders consult their Pentagons, their state departments, their information agencies, and their natural science advisory boards, and come up with a judgment on how any proposed measure of arms control would affect their nation's over-all military and diplomatic posture in the world.

In the case of orbiting space vehicles, there is at least a strong suspicion in Washington that control might work to the advantage of the Soviet Union, and that therefore the United States should seek to delay such control if possible without too much damage to the United States in the world-wide battle for men's minds and loyalties.

Why would control work to the United States' disadvantage? A prohibition of military uses of orbiting objects would rule out the reconnaissance satellite, for one thing. This would be a relatively slight disadvantage to the Soviet Union, because much of the West is already an open book. But it would be a severe blow to Western hopes of breaking through the intelligence barriers thrown up by the Iron Curtain.

Another way in which space can be put to use—by means of projectiles—is seen as an entirely different matter.

Missiles, whether intercontinental or intermediate, are really nothing more than extraordinarily long-range artillery, it is said. The fact that some can be launched from above the ground and others from below the surface of the sea makes them a novel kind of artillery but does not change their fundamental character, experts believe.

Because ballistic missiles are spectacular—traveling thousands of miles in a few minutes—they catch the public eye. The elimination of the danger they pose is what the average person means when he speaks of space-weapon control.

To the military man, elimination of such weapons would improve materially the prospects of defense against surprise attack. Planes and air-breathing missiles are much slower than ballistic missiles. Interception is much easier.

The Soviet Union has proposed that intercontinental missiles be prohibited. It has portrayed this proposal as a sacrifice of Soviet advantage, demanding that, in return, the United States abandon its system of airplane and intermediate-range-missile bases around the periphery of the Soviet empire.

The intercontinental ballistic missile, Moscow argues, is the strategic counterpart of the American bomber and IRBM. If one is to be eliminated, says the Kremlin, the other must be also. In effect, the Soviets are trying to convert their lead in missile technology into bargaining currency and purchase with it the disintegration of the United States military alliances.

The United States rejects any such transaction, in part because the Soviet missile lead may well be overcome if the race continues, and in part because of doubt that a prohibition of ballistic missiles could be made airtight. In addition to the difficulty of detecting hidden launching platforms, there is the fact that launching equipment for peaceful purposes could be converted without too much trouble in case of war, if the necessary missiles had been hidden away.

Meanwhile, lesser measures to reduce the danger of surprise attack, whether by plane or by missile, could be taken, it is pointed out. Elimination of surprise is considered one of the most likely areas of practical action for the near future.

The country or alliance most likely to be the victim of a surprise attack would be the side which would benefit most from such a step. Measures of this kind, therefore, are regarded as concessions by the Soviet Union to the West, which the West presumably would have to purchase by concessions to Moscow.

2.

All the possibilities for arm control require resources of integrity and good will that the Soviet leaders have not yet demonstrated. There seems no doubt, however, that Soviet public opinion stands wholeheartedly for peace. The country's losses during World War II, which only now have become known, were larger than that of any other great nation; proportionally they exceeded the losses suffered by both sides in the American Civil War. To talk peace under these circumstances was a natural for the Soviet leaders.

Stalin, who harnessed the international peace movement to the Communist band wagon and underpinned it through world peace rallies, peace councils, and committees everywhere, certainly had an ulterior motive. In his last speech he referred to the world peace movement as ancillary to the Communist party.

The spell under which he held his people was such that in the name of peace he could have led the Soviet Union into a war.

His successors, whether Nikita S. Khrushchev or those who come after him, will have to maneuver with utmost care to secure popular support for a war which smacks in the least of provocation or aggression.

European observers who know the Soviet Union intimately doubt, moreover, that the Soviet leaders plan for war. In a country where manpower is short, mobilization would slow down or stop entire industries.

Armament expenditures already weigh more heavily on the Soviet economy than they do on the economy of the

United States. A war would stop economic development and risk annihilating what has been rebuilt at unimaginable sacrifice.

There also are political considerations. War would strain the hierarchic and bureaucratic structure of the Soviet state, which only now is beginning to evolve toward something resembling intricate corporate controls. Under the new system, tens of thousands of talented people are encouraged to display initiative. It may take years before they are accustomed to operating as a team.

Decentralization of industrial management, which has vested vast powers in provincial agencies, has enhanced the centrifugal tendencies. The diversity inside the Communist camp, the latent differences of interest between Moscow and Peking, the complex division of labor now being developed among the socialist nations for the time being, also tend to make the Soviet Union vulnerable in case of war.

It has been said often—and by no means only in the United States—that the Soviet Union may be plunged some day into war by domestic developments. Rivalries for power between members of the Presidium (the former Politburo) or the threat of an incipient revolt against the regime are the most frequently mentioned circumstances in which this could happen.

Neither of these circumstances can be ruled out categorically, but neither appears likely.

Rivalries between Presidium members do exist and have existed ever since Lenin's passing; actually, they started even before then, when Lenin became incapacitated. But the record proves that these struggles for the top place, though ruthless, were strictly intramural fights.

Within the ten-year period of 1925-34 Stalin eliminated about a dozen rivals; his heirs eliminated Lavrenti P. Beria in 1953; Nikita S. Khrushchev removed his rivals between 1955 and June, 1957. And all this was accomplished without affecting the conduct of Soviet foreign policy one way or the other.

Nor is there any tangible evidence of the Soviet people becoming so dissatisfied with their regime that they may think of rising against it. Most of the evidence points in the opposite direction, namely, that the Soviet people give credit to their government for an improvement in their living standards, a limited but undeniable restoration of due processes of law, and some other small, but still measurable, benefits.

Recent Western visitors to the Soviet Union also have agreed, virtually without exception, that four decades of propaganda and indoctrination have had their effect on the Soviet people.

Their picture of the free world is gravely distorted. The masses lack any opportunity to obtain unbiased information about the non-Communist world, and the few who are allowed to go abroad are not only tried and tested party members, but also persons with a vested interest in the regime.

Both they and their government, however, despite the Kremlin's aggressiveness in words, seem far from eager to start a war.

At the nineteenth Soviet Communist Party Congress in 1953, the last congress Stalin attended, the Soviet strategic master plan was unfolded for everybody to see.

That plan said clearly that the Soviet Union did not expect to become involved in war, but planned to conquer as the result of growing differences in and the eventual break-up of the Western camp.

There was a great deal of wishful thinking in the forecasts made by Stalin and Georgi M. Malenkov in 1953; they also betrayed Soviet ignorance of the forces that hold the free world together and of the rules under which it operates.

But in the intervening period the passive program of waiting for the free world to fall apart and fall piecemeal into Moscow's lap has been complemented by an active program of economic penetration in Asian, African, and Latin-American countries.

As in the days of the czars, the ruble has begun to roll, and, in the few years since the Soviet economic offensive started, it has brought the Kremlin returns that must not be minimized.

Whether the Soviet economy is strong enough to sustain the ruble offensive indefinitely is questionable. But most diplomatic observers agree that the West should make the best possible effort to meet Moscow's challenge in the field of foreign aid and to meet it with imagination and dispatch.

The one thing the history of the past forty years has taught the world is that where living standards rise, the prospects of communism drop. In the long run this may apply even to the Soviet Union.

3.

Meanwhile, the West is seeking, through collective security and foreign aid, to preserve a peaceful balance for the future. If you draw a line on the map from the United States to every nation with which the United States in 1958 had formal treaty ties, you will draw forty-four big black lines.

And you would conclude—correctly—that Americans have come a long way in the postwar era from the dictum of their founding fathers against entangling alliances.

These bilateral and multilateral commitments did not spring into being at American initiative. They were and are a reaction to a long series of Communist actions, such as pressure on Iran, territorial demands on Turkey, guerrilla and civil war in Greece, seizure of the Balkan nations, the *coup d'état* in Czechoslovakia, rejection of the Marshall Plan, organization of the Cominform, violations of the Potsdam agreement, the Berlin blockade, maintenance of large, threatening Soviet armed forces, building up of satellite forces, and the abuse of the veto in the UN.

The first step toward Western collective security emerged in 1949 as the now-familiar North Atlantic Treaty Organization. By 1952 it stretched from Iceland and Norway on the northern edge of Europe to Greece and Turkey in the south. It is doubtless the strongest peacetime alliance in history.

The Southeast Asia Treaty Organization (SEATO), the Baghdad Pact, and the 1947 Rio treaty are other significant defense groupings. But the pattern of NATO appears to have particular meaning for the future.

The urgency behind this great forward push on freedom's front was simply that of security. But both the moral nature of the peoples it unified, and the economic and political conditions in which the effort took place, made certain that the aims of NATO could never be purely military.

Even its natural antecedents were other than military: the 1947 Truman Doctrine of aid to Greece and Turkey, the Marshall Plan, the Organization for European Economic Cooperation, the European Payments Union, the Council of Europe, the Schuman Plan for a European Coal and Steel Community.

All these plans and movements were contributing to American and European security and unity when NATO appeared as a hard core, backed by irrevocable pledges, for the Atlantic community.

Its task of maintaining integrated military forces and of developing other aspects of collective security was unprecedented. To do these things in peacetime, and in a period when defense had to be political and economic as well as military, required NATO itself to be much more than a military alliance.

It had to develop a sort of civilian "government" which would reflect the views of all the allied governments. It had to find new means for surmounting the obstacles national sovereignty might place in the way of national security. Yet it had to preserve the sovereignty of each nation intact, from that of the United States to that of Iceland and Luxembourg.

It had meanwhile to reach into the national affairs of its members in a way that no international organization had ever been permitted to do before, in peace or even in war. And in Article II of the North Atlantic Treaty, it had authority to promote desirable economic, social and political conditions throughout the new community.

Today these aims bring together members of parliaments from most Western countries in regular meetings. They also send out over the Western world scholars, journalists, and other writers and artists, teachers, and students, who visit one another's countries not quite as foreigners but as fellow members of a new world community.

The vast defense network and the growing social, political, and cultural implications of NATO are only part of the Atlantic community story. Behind the shield that the alliance has provided against aggression, a number of important new ventures in Western unity have been launched. The European Common Market is one. Euratom, the European atom pool, is another.

The sense of community grows out of the day-to-day necessities and contacts among the peoples of the alliance. These do not yet touch the millions directly. But they mold the thousands.

By no means all the contacts are at military levels. Even

those that occur in military duty are promoting a personal
camaraderie that promises to continue in whatever circumstances or professions allied soldiers may meet in years to
come. Officers who work together at the Supreme Headquarters Allied Powers Europe (SHAPE) say they develop
a new outlook which transcends the purely national one
that they brought there when they came.

The children of personnel in alliance organizations go to
school together though they are of many different nation-
alities. In Luxembourg there is a high school for children
of the officials and staff of the European Coal and Steel Community representing six European countries. It uses an international curriculum governed to some extent by the entrance
requirements of universities in the six countries; but the universities are also reported modifying their requirements to
be more in line with the needs of the international school.
And so the feeling for community deepens while it widens.

So many things have happened to bring Western peoples
together in the years since World War II that to recount them
without qualification tends to produce a complacency that
would be quite unjustified.

The trend to unity has suddenly and utterly transformed
Western Europe. It is today unrecognizable as the same place
as Europe, 1948. Its wealth has doubled. Its people have
work. It is gay. It is confident.

Yet at this time in 1958 the politicians and the peoples of
Western Europe are locked in the most serious discussions
about the future.

Can they go on together? Must they part?

Half of Europe thinks it should resolutely set a course to
complete union and press on until it gets there. The other
half thinks it may well be better to travel hopefully than to

arrive—particularly if arrival means the loss of national independence.

This being so, the two halves were almost bound to part company when the goal of unity was seen ahead on the horizon. And it can be seen now.

But can they afford to part?

This is the challenge that faces Western Europe today. This is what the discussions are all about rather than just the respective merits of a common market and a free trade area.

Britain promotes the free trade area as a means of going further toward union without going too far and reaching it. It needs the rest of Europe as much as it cherishes its independence.

"The Europe of six"—France, Belgium, the Netherlands, Luxembourg, Italy, and West Germany—are joined already by treaty in the common market with the goal of eventual union clearly in sight.

But even for them union of the six itself is not enough. They must have Britain, if not inside Europe, at least touching Europe, as close as is imaginatively possible, for their own sakes.

For, if the common market split Europe in two, it would undo much of the progress Western Europe has made in the past ten years.

That progress, one recalls, was made by seventeen nations, not just by six.

It began following General George C. Marshall's speech at Harvard on June 5, 1947, offering help to European countries if they would get together to help themselves.

The Organization for European Economic Cooperation was formed in 1948. National recovery programs were coordinated and United States aid divided according to need.

An attack began on quotas. Members were required to

free from quotas first 50 per cent and eventually 90 per cent of goods imported on private account.

In 1950 the European Payments Union was set up. In 1951 a code of liberalization of trade and invisible transactions was adopted. Technical information centers were established throughout Europe.

Progress was rapid. Business boomed.

Within six years it had become clear, in the OEEC's own words, "that liberalization in its present form has practically reached the limits of its possibilities."

Simple cooperation was no longer enough.

Not merely did Europe have to go on if the momentum that made progress possible was to be maintained, but it had to go beyond cooperation for reasons of practical detail.

It is very probable that in the modern world economic unity won't work without political unity. That is really what the OEEC itself has been saying. But economic unity has got to be made to work, if possible. It is important and perhaps vital to Europe's 260 million people and to their hopes for wider opportunities, enlarged freedoms, better living, and continued influence.

4.

In the meantime, the less privileged countries all over the world are receiving aid from the more privileged. Some look to the Soviet Union and its increased economic activities. More look to the West.

Consider the British Commonwealth, the empire that grew up. It covers a quarter of all the world's land surface and contains a quarter of all the world's people. Most of the land surface is "underdeveloped." Most of the 650 million people are still hungry. Yet the land produces more than half the world's precious metals, one-third of its precious stones, nearly half its rice and half its wool, and one-quarter of its wheat and sugar.

But the land needs capital; the people need jobs; the jobs demand industries.

The main agencies supplying these in varying measures are:

1. The Colombo Plan.
2. The Foundation for Mutual Assistance in Africa South of the Sahara.
3. The International Bank for Reconstruction and Development.
4. Development Finance Corporations, both international and local.
5. The Colonial Development Corporation.
6. Commercial companies.
7. Private investors on the London capital market.

Total British aid alone to the Commonwealth—which used to be British—in the five years to 1958 had topped 1 billion pounds (2.8 billion dollars).

Seventy per cent of the new capital invested in the sterling Commonwealth since 1947 has come from Britain, 15 per cent from the United States, 10 per cent from the International Bank, and 5 per cent from other sources. (Canada, although a Commonwealth member, is not included in the "sterling Commonwealth," being a dollar country.)

Private investment, by companies and individuals, accounts for more than half the total.

A very important new field of cooperation is opening up in the development of nuclear energy for peaceful purposes. Canada and Britain are naturally the leading partners at the moment. India and Britain, however, recently signed a mutual assistance agreement and there are regular connections being established between almost all Commonwealth countries.

But it now is becoming clear that just as independence was itself not enough for progress, so aid alone is not enough. Even mutual aid.

Economic progress derives from production and from trade. In the West as a whole, the big shift in foreign aid these days is toward loans and credits instead of gifts and grants, toward many-nation participation (which thus draws on the total resources of the free world), and toward expanded functions by the big international banking organizations, such as the World Bank and the International Monetary Fund.

The United States Congress in 1958 looked favorably toward such ways of improving foreign aid when it approved a four-year extension of the reciprocal trade program.

Most certainly, the United States foreign-aid program can be set down as having been an effective instrument for peace since World War II in bolstering the sturdy independence of fledgling nations and in combating the economic inroads of the Soviet bloc.

It is also true that, in its earlier phases, foreign aid was sometimes ineffectually administered. There were impractical projects; there were scatter-blast plans which made no real improvement in a country; there were unskilled administrators.

The military-aid programs have been generally effective. They have kept Turkey's economic structure from collapsing under the weight of a necessarily swollen army. They helped build a fighting force out of the South Korean Army, which North Korea profoundly respects. Stepped-up funds to Generalissimo Chiang Kai-shek's Nationalist forces have kept up Formosa's morale.

The United States has poured more than a billion dollars into Nationalist China, since its government fled to Formosa from the mainland in 1949, in both military and economic aid.

Generally speaking, the business of bulwarking the defenses of key military allies maintaining large forces, such as Nationalist China, South Korea, South Vietnam, and Turkey, has accounted for 70 per cent of the total foreign-aid bill in recent years, or since the Marshall Plan—which was primarily economic—came to an end.

There are many special categories of foreign aid. The farm-surplus-disposal program is available for sending surplus wheat, cotton, or other farm products abroad, where they are paid for by local currencies. Congress added 2.25 billion dollars in new authorizations to this program in 1958.

Mr. Eisenhower's atoms-for-peace fund (5.5 million dollars) helps finance up to one-half the cost of research reactors in friendly countries. The United States contributes additional millions to refugee programs, to the UN Children's Fund, and to UN-administered foreign aid.

The Export-Import Bank is busily lending money to foreign countries the world over to finance and stimulate the purchase of American exports. Congress has just added 2 billion dollars to its nearly exhausted lending authority of 5 billion dollars.

The United States is the largest contributor to the World Bank, capitalized at 9 billion dollars, which, with a membership of sixty-five free-world nations, lends money for development projects ranging from highways in Ethiopia and railway modernization in Nigeria to hydroelectric plants in Malaya.

The 700-million-dollar United States Development Loan Fund, for making longer-term loans abroad, expected to have

2 billion dollars' worth of new applications on its desk by mid-1959.

UN sources say that the United States now is spending approximately 5 billion dollars annually in both bilateral and multilateral assistance to underdeveloped countries, and has been doing so for several years. Simultaneously, the Soviet Union has been spending about 1.5 billion dollars, according to the UN.

In the eight years to 1959, the United States contributed 22 billion dollars in mutual defense assistance to its free-world allies. During the same period, these allies themselves contributed 141 billion dollars to develop their over-all strength.

Totaling the mammoth effort, Washington reports that since World War II, in the thirteen years ending with 1958, the United States supplied in foreign aid these sums: to Western Europe, 38.4 billion dollars; to the Far East and Pacific, 15.7 billion dollars; to the Near East, Africa, and Southeast Asia, 8.7 billion dollars; to American republics, 2.5 billion dollars.

The total present cost of the mutual security program is 5 per cent of the national budget. Its intimate cost is about five cents a day for every man, woman, and child in the United States, according to State Department figures.

5.

When we get back to the man, woman, and child, we get back to the fundamental factors in the international equation. If nations are to live together, people must live together. National integrity is personal integrity writ large. The world has in the UN a unique instrument for fostering this integrity. Over many millenniums mankind has been seeking ways to beat swords into ploughshares, to heal animosities and adjust differences without recurrent warfare. The UN is the twentieth century's expression of this aspiration.

Few even of its most ardent supporters would claim that the UN has fulfilled all the hopes which were evoked at its birth. Most realistic observers are persuaded, however, that it has made a contribution to the world into which it was plunged.

The UN must contribute; it cannot dictate. It is not a world government. It is nothing more or less than machinery through which sovereign states can do business with one another—that, plus a charter of ideals which serves as a standard of conduct, beckoning and drawing men upward.

The real reason why the UN is unique is that—because of the ideals in the Charter—it can be used much more effectively by the man or nation seeking justice and progress than it can by the man or nation promoting a purely selfish interest.

The power of the UN is the power of world opinion. The man or nation attempting to make use of that power can do so only if he can persuade world opinion his cause is just. For a time, of course, a malefactor may be able to deceive many; but ultimately the facts have a way of coming to the surface.

Andrei Y. Vishinsky, one of the most venomous cold-war spokesmen of the Soviet Union, used to say that "facts are stubborn things." He himself was one of the principal victims of that fact.

On one occasion when the UN General Assembly was meeting in the Palais de Chaillot, Paris, and even the marble statues in the corridors of that erstwhile museum seemed to shudder at the verbal thunder, Mr. Vishinsky tried to persuade the other delegates that it was "nonsense" to talk of the Soviet Union exporting revolution.

"Imagine!" he said, in effect—his precise words escape memory—"What a fantastic idea. I can see that you are amused by it, too. There is Prince Wan [the Foreign Minister of Thailand] smiling. He knows what nonsense it is."

Prince Wan, whose country had had much opportunity to observe the attempted export of Communist revolution, both by the Soviet Union and by Communist China, sought the floor when the white-haired man from Moscow had finished.

"It is dangerous for Mr. Vishinsky to interpret my smiles," he said in the soft, gentle tones of the Orient. "I always smile."

Much of the diplomacy at the UN takes place behind the scenes, in corridors, private offices, and lounges, or at social affairs. Some UN people estimate that 85 to 90 per cent of their meaningful work is done in private.

Decisions made privately are later spread on the public record to give them official sanction and added lasting quality. It is as if the script for a complicated drama—a melodrama, it sometimes seems—were to be written, rewritten, and rehearsed behind drawn curtains, then presented to the public.

Not all public sessions of the UN, however, are mere recitations of lines prepared in advance. When private negotiation reaches an impasse, the role of the debate thereafter is quite different.

It then is an effort by the respective adversaries to improve their bargaining positions by appeals to world opinion. The party which is most successful in persuading world opinion of the rectitude of its stand mobilizes corresponding pressure on the other to be more reasonable.

Such pressures have noticeable effect on all countries, including even dictatorships which would like the world to believe they are invulnerable to moral sanctions. In practice, they clearly are not.

6.

Moral and spiritual strength must be utilized by all of us if the future is to bring freedom from war. A radical approach will be needed.

Peace is too often a condition that you seek to impose on the other fellow.

One nation, or a group of "powers," as they significantly are called, keeps order and the others perforce agree. There is quiet for awhile, and then someone rebels.

Historically, this kind of peace does not last. It is clearly inadequate for the present.

There are signs today that a new concept of peace is winning favor. It begins with mastery of one's self, and only then proceeds to the restraint of someone else.

It springs from a simple, intuitive element of wisdom that ordinary people learn in their home and community affairs: that you are not always right and the other fellow is not always wrong. That evil, at base, is impersonal, and that the fight for peace, the authentic cold war, is part of the conquest over all evil everywhere, in your own country as well as the other fellow's.

Therefore, the war on war begins at home. It exerts a powerful compulsion on the other fellow in today's world when you yourself practice what you preach. You set the example. Then if he has to be restrained, if he is a Hitler of his time and cannot be held in check except by force, and, if arms control has not yet been achieved, you can display force with a good conscience and the rest of the world will approve.

To start struggling within yourself to subdue the forces of war is a revolutionary international concept.

Even in today's world, after great advances in spreading

international law, after the idealism poured into the League of Nations and matured in the UN era, and even after the specter of nuclear war has sobered men and women throughout the world and sharpened their longing for peace, nations still tend to live by a double moral standard. At home, they recognize the power of brotherhood, by and large, and try to live by the basic rule common to all the world's great religions that you should do unto others as you would have them do unto you.

But little attention is paid to an international golden rule.

Nations often proclaim their ideals to the outside world, to be sure, but they tend to act in terms of power. This is the accepted practice, handed down from the past. It continues despite the new efforts in this century to provide world standards of law and conduct and despite important changes in the forms of international maneuver.

But the subject here is not international organization, not charters or the slow, majestic spread of law. We are dealing here with attitudes, with what happens in the minds of men, where the causes of war admittedly lie. It is attitudes and desires, the capacities of men to identify and expose the hidden sources of war in the human mind and subdue them, that give to the forms of international organization their content—or lack of content.

And on this deeper level, where men determine the motives of their actions, there is often a strong negative element of "ism" attached to the positive qualities which are genuinely national. Under the banner of nationalism, pride and power, self-righteousness and anger march aggressively, and your own lapses into primitive attitudes are lost in the brilliance of the onslaught on the enemy. The civilian rarely understands how deeply the diplomat finds himself drawn into the "necessities of power," and the hard dealings which are imposed on him—so it is easy to argue—by the callous or hardened criminal attitude of the other side.

The question now is whether men can do better.

The problem of attitudes now becomes correspondingly much more subtle.

How do you as a diplomat or foreign minister retain a sense of poise and moral balance while you are deep in the business of restraining evil? If you must have a military establishment to defend the freer parts of the world, how can you avoid a certain amount of the military mentality, of that pugnacious, alert pride of strength which will have to rescue you, if all else fails, and which can show the other fellow that force will be met with force and therefore will not pay?

How, as a matter of practical politics, can you arouse your people to the hard, distasteful business of turning peacetime into cold war, in order to avoid nuclear hot war, without appealing to their martial spirit and national pride, and without goading them by the fear of what otherwise would happen?

Is it naïve to talk about living up to your own peacetime ideals, and coping with the negative impulses in your own behavior, when you are standing, armed, on the ramparts of Western society, preoccupied with this stern business of defense? If we had to wait until we were as pure as Sir Galahad, would we ever defend free society?

These are the questions of the hour.

These questions cannot be answered by better international machinery, however good it may be and however much it may help. They are questions of motive and action and can be answered only on the moral level.

Let's face it, we of the West are trying to do two apparently contradictory things in this time of cold war. And much, perhaps most of our trouble, in foreign policy, stems from the resulting clash of attitudes. We are trying to defend society against the brigand element which seems always more threatening in today's world. And at the same time we are trying to behave like decent people so we can let our light shine and attract other people to the way of life we believe in.

One of these tasks is primarily military. The other is primarily humanitarian. We are bedeviled by the fact that each task requires an apparently contradictory set of attitudes and motives, and that we cannot bring ourselves to merge the two —we cannot seem to do both, adequately, at the same time.

What can a frankly moral analysis of this conflict of attitudes contribute? Can it show how to combine strength and affection in foreign policy?

It can. At least it can show in principle how this can be done. And that is the first, indispensable step.

Consider:

On the moral level, each quality in a man's character—and why not in a nation's character?—has both its positive and its negative side.

Strength in its best sense is courage to stand for what one considers right. It is the sinew of a disciplined and efficient mind. It is the firm resolve to combat what one considers to be wrongdoing and to protect people from being pushed around.

No one questions the value of these warrior qualities in their best sense.

But leave these qualities alone, unbalanced by the humanitarian values—and they can rapidly degenerate into the abuse of these very same virtues. Firmness becomes stubbornness and pride. Strength becomes arbitrary power. Defense of freedom becomes defense of self, right or wrong—the defense of special self-interest. The motive becomes partisan and self-centered rather than universal. The human mind, when it goes over from honest strength to the spurious sort, becomes a cynical and ruthless instrument. It spills over into attitudes which are not merely firm—but belligerent, provocative, overbearing. In come anger, self-righteousness, and greed. At its worst the abuse of strength becomes frantic and responds to fear and hatred instead of conviction.

The dividing line between positive strength and its negative abuse is clearly a moral line.

A nation, a diplomat, can cultivate the positive set of attitudes or its reverse.

Consider, now, the other key quality which we find it so hard to square with strength in the foreign policy—that of friendliness. Here, too, there are both plus and minus.

On the positive side, a country which can express compassion in its foreign policy is turning its most attractive face to the outside world. A diplomat who puts friendliness first will not be afraid to show respect for the integrity of others and a lively interest in their hopes and fears. He will listen to them, to see what they have to offer, and not merely talk at them. He will show generosity and be tolerant. He will be slow to take offense, quick to be understanding. He will not be holier or superior.

In the large sense, this is universal love in action. It is the most powerful force of attraction that exists.

But here again, when this quality is allowed to deteriorate to its negative aspect, the result—in the world of public affairs—is weakness. Affection toward others is supplanted by the willingness to indulge weakness or evil in others. Emotional softness in the face of tyranny becomes cowardice, the craven mentality. Idealism becomes visionary. The sharp discrimination between right and wrong is blurred into a naïve and innocent approach toward evil-doing which is credulous and results in appeasement.

Here again the dividing line between the positive virtue and its obverse is a moral dividing line.

A nation, a diplomat, can cultivate authentic brotherhood or its pale shadow.

Now comes the point.

It is possible to mix authentic strength with authentic compassion. It is not possible to mix their negative extremes.

Belligerence is not only the abuse of strength, it is the sworn enemy of affection and inevitably will tend to undermine it.

Likewise, appeasement is not only a misunderstanding of the real meaning of affection; it is the sworn enemy of strength and, if allowed to, will wreck it.

On the positive side, meanwhile, there is solid reason to say that the genuine qualities of firmness and brotherhood need each other. Otherwise each is incomplete and likely to get off the track.

The strong nation in today's world will win friends and use its strength justly if it serves a higher humanitarian purpose. Mere militarism repels.

And the most generous and considerate foreign policy, respecting the needs and desires of other countries and peoples, can survive in the face of today's aggressors only if it is protected and secure.

The path of moral leadership for peace, then, is to discriminate between these good qualities and their opposites, to act on the one and reject the other. On this moral level, the apparent contradiction which harasses the peace efforts of the West melts away. And if the contradiction between strength and decency ceases to exist in our attitudes and thought, it should not be impossible to find specific actions and statements and policies in the day-to-day business of world affairs, to spell out the basic agreement between them.

To come back to the original point.

There are signs that this simple and yet profound concept is beginning to assert itself more demandingly in today's world. Smaller nations are not pushed around as they once were. The powerful are being held up to their responsibilities, and, when they do not act as they require others to act, there is an outcry. It comes from public opinion, and it is a strong force at international conferences and the UN. Respect for even-handed justice and law has spread better than those who live in the diplomatic traditions of the past yet recognize.

If this moral sense continues to grow in world affairs, the nations which best master themselves will exert the best leadership abroad. In place of the self-interest of the narrow kind of nationalism, the trend of the times will be toward an international golden rule. Man's great future will be secure.